THE POWER OF QUANTUM MACHINE LEARNING

WITH TENSORFLOW QUANTUM, QISKIT, PENNYLANE, AND AMAZON BRAKET: FROM ALGORITHMS TO APPLICATIONS

TIMOTHY UGBAJA

ISBN:

DEDICATION

This book is dedicated to my partner, **Stanley Coffey**, whose immeasurable love, unwavering support, and constant encouragement have been my guiding light. Your belief in me has given me purpose and the strength to keep pushing forward, even in the face of challenges. Thank you for being my greatest inspiration and my steadfast companion on this journey.

ABOUT THE BOOK

Title: "THE POWER OF QUANTUM MACHINE LEARNING: With Tensorflow Quantum, Qiskit, Pennylane, And Amazon Braket: From Algorithms To Applications"

This book serves as an authoritative, in-depth resource for anyone seeking to understand and harness the transformative potential of Quantum Machine Learning (QML). As the intersection of quantum computing and artificial intelligence continues to shape the future of technology, this comprehensive guide offers both a theoretical and practical exploration of how quantum algorithms can be applied to revolutionize machine learning paradigms. From fundamental principles to cutting-edge applications, **"Quantum Machine Learning"** provides a roadmap for mastering this emerging field.

Purpose and Scope

Quantum computing promises to accelerate machine learning by providing powerful computational tools that can process vast amounts of data and perform complex calculations exponentially faster than classical systems. This book is designed to bridge the gap between the intricacies of quantum computing and the practical needs of machine learning practitioners. It is intended for a wide range of readers, from newcomers to quantum computing and AI enthusiasts, to advanced researchers and professionals seeking to explore the impact of quantum technologies on machine learning.

The book covers key theoretical concepts such as quantum mechanics, quantum algorithms, and quantum programming languages, along with in-depth insights into their application to real-world machine learning problems. It further examines how quantum computing can be integrated with traditional AI models, providing hybrid approaches that maximize performance and scalability. Practical case studies and step-by-step tutorials are included to illustrate the application of quantum-enhanced machine learning in various industries, such as finance, healthcare, logistics, and more.

What You Will Learn:

1. **Fundamentals of Quantum Computing**: Gain a solid foundation in quantum mechanics, qubits, quantum gates, and the principles that govern quantum systems. Understand the key differences between classical and quantum computing, and how these differences open new avenues for machine learning applications.
2. **Quantum Machine Learning Algorithms**: Explore key quantum algorithms such as Quantum Support Vector Machines (QSVM), Quantum Neural Networks (QNNs), and Quantum Principal Component Analysis (qPCA). Learn how these

algorithms outperform their classical counterparts for specific machine learning tasks, like classification, clustering, and regression.

3. **Integrating Quantum and Classical Systems**: Discover hybrid models that combine classical machine learning methods with quantum computing to optimize performance for complex tasks. Learn how to structure workflows that maximize the strengths of both systems while addressing the limitations of each.
4. **Applications Across Industries**: Understand the transformative potential of QML in various sectors, including finance (for portfolio optimization and risk analysis), healthcare (for drug discovery and genomics), and logistics (for optimization of supply chains). Explore real-world case studies that demonstrate how QML is already starting to impact these industries.
5. **Scalability and Practical Deployment**: Learn the challenges of scaling quantum machine learning solutions, from addressing quantum hardware limitations to optimizing quantum circuits for large-scale applications. Discover how to navigate the complexities of quantum resource management and ensure your solutions can scale in real-world environments.
6. **Ethical and Practical Considerations**: Delve into the ethical implications of deploying quantum-powered AI, addressing concerns such as accessibility, security, and the societal impact of automation. Develop a thoughtful framework for considering the practical issues of QML adoption and deployment, from technical to ethical challenges.
7. **Building a Career in QML**: This book also includes valuable advice for aspiring professionals, researchers, and entrepreneurs seeking to build careers or businesses in the rapidly evolving QML field. Gain insights into opportunities for innovation, collaboration, and research in the QML ecosystem, and learn how to position yourself at the forefront of this revolutionary technology.

Who This Book Is For:

This book is ideal for anyone interested in exploring the intersection of quantum computing and machine learning. It is well-suited for:

- **AI and Data Science Professionals**: Who want to understand how quantum computing can enhance machine learning tasks and improve model performance.
- **Quantum Computing Enthusiasts**: Who wish to learn how quantum technologies are applied to machine learning and gain insight into the practical side of QML.
- **Researchers and Academics**: Looking for a detailed and thorough guide to explore QML from both a theoretical and practical perspective, with the goal of advancing knowledge in the field.
- **Entrepreneurs and Innovators**: Interested in leveraging QML for creating innovative products, platforms, or services that disrupt industries and address real-world challenges.

Why This Book Matters:

As quantum computing continues to mature, its potential to revolutionize machine learning and AI grows exponentially. The synergy between quantum and classical approaches in machine learning promises to accelerate progress in data science, optimization, and artificial intelligence in ways previously thought unattainable. This book offers readers the tools, knowledge, and practical frameworks to understand and implement quantum machine learning solutions, positioning them to contribute to a future where QML is a cornerstone of technological innovation.

Table of Contents

PREFACE

We are living through the dawn of a new computational era—one that promises to reshape not only how we think about machines and algorithms, but also how we understand the very nature of intelligence, complexity, and possibility. At the intersection of two of the most revolutionary fields in modern science—**quantum computing** and **machine learning**—emerges a powerful frontier: **Quantum Machine Learning (QML)**.

This book was born from a sense of urgency and wonder. Urgency because the pace of technological change demands a new generation of thinkers and builders who are not merely consumers of AI, but architects of what comes next. Wonder because quantum computing, once considered the province of theoretical physicists, is now entering practical territory, empowering us to tackle problems that were previously unsolvable—even by the world's most advanced supercomputers.

When I first began exploring quantum computing, it felt like learning to program in an alien language governed by probabilistic logic, entangled states, and multidimensional spaces. Layering that onto machine learning, which itself is complex and ever-evolving, seemed daunting at first. But soon, I realized: the future of intelligent systems depends on bridging these two worlds.

This book is the bridge I wish I had when I started.

Whether you are a data scientist curious about quantum acceleration, a researcher developing hybrid algorithms, an engineer working with Qiskit or TensorFlow Quantum, or simply a curious mind standing at the edge of what's possible—you'll find both a **theoretical foundation** and **practical guidance** here. We'll explore the frameworks (TFQ, Qiskit, PennyLane, Amazon Braket), dive into real-world use cases, and, perhaps most importantly, reimagine what machine learning can do when it's powered by quantum logic.

But this book is not just about tools and code. It is about **vision**. It's about preparing for a world where quantum-enhanced AI revolutionizes industries—from drug discovery to logistics, from finance to climate modeling—and where today's learners become tomorrow's pioneers.

You don't need a Ph.D. in physics or computer science to benefit from this journey. What you need is a willingness to learn, explore, and challenge the boundaries of what you thought technology could do.

Welcome to the next chapter in computing.
Let's build the future—qubit by qubit.

Timothy Ugbaja
Author
2025

PART 1: Fundamentals of Quantum Computing and Machine Learning

Part 1: Foundations of Quantum Computing and Machine Learning introduces readers to the essential building blocks of quantum computing and classical machine learning, setting the stage for their convergence. Beginning with an exploration of key quantum concepts—such as qubits, superposition, entanglement, and quantum gates—readers will gain a clear understanding of how quantum systems operate. The section then transitions into a review of classical machine learning fundamentals, including supervised and unsupervised learning, neural networks, and deep learning frameworks. Finally, the chapters bridge these two domains, explaining how quantum principles can revolutionize traditional machine learning techniques and why quantum machine learning is poised to solve challenges beyond the capabilities of classical approaches. This foundational knowledge ensures readers, regardless of prior expertise, are equipped to grasp the advanced concepts and applications that follow.

CHAPTER 1: Introduction to Quantum Computing

DESCRIPTION:

This chapter introduces readers to the core concepts of quantum computing, explaining the fundamental principles that differentiate it from classical computing. Readers will explore topics like qubits, superposition, entanglement, and quantum gates, building a solid understanding of how quantum systems work. By the end of this chapter, readers will have a clear grasp of the foundational ideas needed to understand and apply quantum computing in machine learning contexts.

What is Quantum Computing?

Quantum computing represents a monumental leap in computational paradigms, moving beyond the limitations of classical computing to harness the principles of quantum mechanics. At its core, quantum computing is not merely an incremental improvement to traditional computing—it's a transformational shift that redefines how we process information, solve problems, and approach complexity in the digital age.

Key Differences Between Classical and Quantum Computing

To understand quantum computing, we must first appreciate how it differs fundamentally from classical computing:

1. **Classical Computing: The Binary Foundation**
   Classical computers, the ones powering everything from smartphones to supercomputers, rely on **bits** as their fundamental unit of information. These bits operate in a binary state—either `0` or `1`. Through a combination of billions of these binary states, classical computers perform calculations, execute programs, and store data.

   This binary system, while extraordinarily powerful, is constrained by the linear nature of computation. Classical computers process one state or operation at a time, even when distributed across many processors.

2. **Quantum Computing: The Qubit Revolution**
   Quantum computing, by contrast, relies on **quantum bits**, or **qubits**. Qubits are fundamentally different because they leverage the principles of quantum mechanics—specifically, **superposition** and **entanglement**—to represent and process information in ways that classical bits cannot.
   - **Superposition:** Unlike classical bits that are strictly `0` or `1`, qubits can exist in a superposition of both `0` and `1` simultaneously. This means that a quantum computer can explore multiple possible states or solutions at once, exponentially increasing its computational potential.
   - **Entanglement:** Qubits can also become entangled, meaning the state of one qubit is directly correlated with the state of another, no matter how far apart they are.

This property allows quantum computers to process and share information in ways that defy classical logic.

The Fundamental Motivation for Quantum Computing

Why do we need quantum computing when classical computers already excel in so many areas? The answer lies in **complexity** and the inherent limitations of classical systems when faced with certain types of problems.

1. **Classical Bottlenecks**
   Classical computers struggle with problems that grow exponentially in complexity. Tasks like factoring large numbers (important for cryptography), simulating molecular interactions (critical for drug discovery), or optimizing massive systems (like global logistics) require immense computational power. These problems often fall into the category of "intractable" for classical machines, meaning they would take an unreasonable amount of time—sometimes longer than the age of the universe—to solve.
2. **Quantum Advantage**
   Quantum computers, by leveraging superposition, entanglement, and quantum interference, have the potential to solve these intractable problems exponentially faster than their classical counterparts. For example:
   - **Cryptography:** Shor's algorithm, a quantum algorithm, can factorize large numbers exponentially faster than the best-known classical algorithms, threatening current encryption methods.
   - **Chemistry and Materials Science:** Quantum computers can simulate molecular and atomic interactions with unparalleled precision, paving the way for breakthroughs in drug development, energy storage, and materials engineering.
   - **Optimization Problems:** Quantum systems excel at exploring vast solution spaces simultaneously, making them ideal for solving optimization challenges in finance, logistics, and machine learning.

Quantum Computing's Role in Solving Complex Problems

The true power of quantum computing lies in its ability to tackle problems previously considered unsolvable. While classical computers excel at linear problem-solving, quantum computers thrive in environments where the relationships between variables are highly complex and interconnected.

1. **Real-World Impact**
   Imagine trying to simulate the behavior of a complex molecule to design a new drug. A classical supercomputer might require years to calculate all possible interactions between electrons and atoms. A quantum computer, on the other hand, can model these interactions in minutes, unlocking new possibilities in healthcare and medicine.

   Similarly, optimizing supply chains, designing next-generation AI algorithms, or understanding fundamental physics could become feasible on a scale never before imagined.

2. **Hybrid Potential**
   It's important to note that quantum computers won't entirely replace classical computers. Instead, they will augment them. By working together in hybrid quantum-classical systems, we can solve problems with both precision and scalability. Quantum computing will handle the heavy lifting for highly complex calculations, while classical systems manage more routine tasks.

The Promise of Quantum Computing

Quantum computing is not a distant dream—it's an emerging reality. Companies like IBM, Google, and Amazon, along with frameworks like TensorFlow Quantum, Qiskit, PennyLane, and Amazon Braket, are making quantum computing more accessible to researchers, engineers, and developers.

While we are still in the early stages of its development, the promise of quantum computing is clear: it has the potential to redefine industries, solve humanity's grandest challenges, and usher in a new era of technological innovation.

Understanding quantum computing is no longer optional for those seeking to stay at the forefront of science and technology. It's the foundation for the next wave of breakthroughs—and this chapter is your gateway to that transformative journey.

Qubits: The Building Blocks of Quantum Computing

In the realm of quantum computing, **qubits** (short for *quantum bits*) are the fundamental units of information, akin to classical bits in traditional computing. However, while classical bits are binary and can only exist in a state of `0` or `1`, qubits leverage the principles of **quantum mechanics** to unlock new dimensions of computation. This distinction is the cornerstone of quantum computing's revolutionary power, enabling the exploration of complex problems that are insurmountable for classical systems.

What Are Qubits?

A **qubit** is a quantum system that encodes information in a quantum state. Unlike a classical bit that exists in one of two discrete states (`0` or `1`), a qubit can exist in a **superposition** of both states simultaneously. This means that a qubit is not limited to processing one piece of information at a time; instead, it can represent and process multiple possibilities simultaneously.

Qubits are realized through various physical systems, such as:

- **Photon Polarization:** Encoding qubits in the horizontal ($|H\rangle$) or vertical ($|V\rangle$) polarization of light.
- **Electron Spins:** Using the spin-up ($|\uparrow\rangle$) or spin-down ($|\downarrow\rangle$) states of an electron.
- **Superconducting Circuits:** Leveraging electrical currents in superconducting loops.

Each of these implementations relies on the unique properties of quantum mechanics, which allow qubits to behave in ways that classical bits cannot.

How Do Qubits Differ from Classical Bits?

To appreciate the transformative power of qubits, it's essential to understand how they fundamentally differ from classical bits:

1. **Binary vs. Quantum States**
   - A classical bit is binary: it can be either `0` or `1`, and at any given moment, it exists in one of these two states.
   - A qubit exists in a quantum state, which is a complex combination of `0` and `1`. This combination is described mathematically as a **linear superposition** of the two states:

     $$|\psi\rangle = \alpha|0\rangle + \beta|1\rangle$$

     Here, α and β are complex numbers, and their squared magnitudes ($|\alpha|^2$ *and* $|\beta|^2$) represent the probabilities of measuring the qubit in the states `0` and `1`, respectively.

2. **Superposition**
   - Superposition allows a qubit to be in multiple states simultaneously. For example, a single qubit can represent both `0` and `1` at the same time, enabling parallel computation.
   - This is fundamentally different from a classical bit, which can only hold one value at a time. Superposition is what gives quantum computers their exponential scaling potential.
3. **Entanglement**
   - Qubits can become **entangled**, meaning the state of one qubit is intrinsically linked to the state of another, regardless of the distance between them. This creates correlations that classical systems cannot replicate.
   - Entanglement enables quantum computers to process and transmit information in profoundly interconnected ways, which is crucial for tasks like quantum cryptography and distributed computing.
4. **Measurement**
   - When you measure a qubit, its quantum state "collapses" to one of the classical states (`0` or `1`) based on the probabilities determined by $|\alpha|^2$ *and* $|\beta|^2$.
   - This probabilistic nature of measurement contrasts with classical systems, where the state of a bit is deterministic and known.

Understanding Quantum States, Superposition, and Measurement

1. **Quantum States**
    - The state of a qubit is a vector in a two-dimensional complex vector space, represented as $|\psi\rangle = \alpha|0\rangle + \beta|1\rangle$.
    - The quantum state contains all the information about the qubit, and its behavior is governed by the **principles of quantum mechanics**.
2. **Superposition**
    - In superposition, a qubit doesn't "choose" between `0` and `1`—it exists in a combination of both until measured. For example, a qubit in the state $\frac{1}{\sqrt{2}}|0\rangle + \frac{1}{\sqrt{2}}|1\rangle$ has equal probabilities of being measured as `0` or `1`.
    - Superposition enables quantum computers to process multiple possibilities at once, exponentially increasing their computational power compared to classical systems.
3. **Measurement**
    - When a qubit is measured, its state collapses into one of the two classical states (`0` or `1`), based on the probabilities defined by its quantum state.
    - For example, if $|\psi\rangle = 0.8|0\rangle + 0.6|1\rangle$, then the qubit has a $0.8^2 = 64\%$ chance of being measured as `0` and a $0.6^2 = 36\%$ chance of being measured as `1`.
    - Measurement disrupts the quantum state, meaning the original superposition is lost once observed. This is a critical distinction from classical bits, which can be read repeatedly without altering their state.

The Power of Qubits in Quantum Computing

The unique properties of qubits—**superposition, entanglement, and probabilistic measurement**—allow quantum computers to perform computations in ways that classical computers cannot replicate.

1. **Parallelism Through Superposition**
    - A single qubit in superposition can encode two states simultaneously. Two qubits can encode four states, three qubits can encode eight states, and so on.
    - For *n* qubits, a quantum system can process 2^n states at once, enabling exponential parallelism.

2. **Correlations Through Entanglement**
   - Entanglement allows quantum computers to process interconnected data and solve problems where the relationships between variables are highly complex.
3. **Solving Intractable Problems**
   - Qubits enable quantum algorithms to explore vast solution spaces efficiently, solving problems like factoring large numbers, optimizing supply chains, and simulating quantum systems far faster than classical systems.

Challenges of Qubits

While qubits are powerful, they are also fragile and difficult to control:

1. **Decoherence:** Qubits are sensitive to environmental noise, which can disrupt their quantum state.
2. **Error Correction:** Maintaining accurate qubit states requires sophisticated error-correction methods, as quantum information is inherently probabilistic.
3. **Scalability:** Building large-scale quantum systems with many reliable qubits is an ongoing challenge in the field.

Qubits are the foundation of quantum computing, offering a paradigm shift in how we process and store information. By leveraging the principles of **superposition, entanglement, and probabilistic measurement**, qubits open the door to solving problems that are fundamentally beyond the reach of classical computers. Understanding qubits is essential for anyone looking to harness the transformative potential of quantum computing—and this chapter has provided the foundational knowledge to begin that journey.

Quantum Entanglement and Superposition

Quantum computing is rooted in phenomena that defy classical intuition, two of the most fundamental being **quantum superposition** and **quantum entanglement**. These principles, derived from the fabric of quantum mechanics, are the cornerstone of quantum computing's unparalleled capabilities. Together, they enable quantum systems to perform computations that classical computers cannot replicate, giving rise to **quantum parallelism**, a defining feature of quantum computational power.

Quantum Superposition: Exploring the Multitude of Possibilities

At the heart of quantum mechanics lies the concept of **superposition**, the idea that a quantum system can exist in multiple states simultaneously until observed or measured. In the context of quantum computing, this means a single **qubit** can represent a combination of the classical states `0` and `1` at the same time.

1. **Mathematical Representation of Superposition**
   A qubit's state is expressed as a **quantum state vector**:

   $$|\psi\rangle = \alpha|0\rangle + \beta|1\rangle$$

   Here:

   - $|0\rangle$ *and* $|1\rangle$ represent the basis states, analogous to the classical binary states.
   - α *and* β are complex numbers that determine the probabilities of measuring the qubit in state `0` or `1`, where $|\alpha|^2 + |\beta|^2 = 1$.
2. **Implications of Superposition**
   - Superposition enables quantum systems to process multiple possibilities simultaneously. For example, a system of *n* qubits in superposition can represent 2^n possible states at once.
   - Unlike classical bits, which encode one state at a time, qubits in superposition exponentially expand the computational space. This ability forms the foundation of quantum algorithms, allowing them to explore vast solution spaces efficiently.
3. **Measurement and Collapse**
   - When a qubit in superposition is measured, it collapses to one of the basis states, `0` or `1`, with probabilities defined by $|\alpha|^2$ *and* $|\beta|^2$.
   - This collapse reflects the probabilistic nature of quantum mechanics, contrasting with the deterministic behavior of classical systems.

Quantum Entanglement: Correlations Beyond Classical Limits

Entanglement is a uniquely quantum phenomenon in which two or more qubits become inextricably linked, such that the state of one qubit cannot be described independently of the state of the other(s), no matter how far apart they are. Albert Einstein famously referred to entanglement as "spooky action at a distance," highlighting its non-classical and counterintuitive nature.

1. **Definition of Entanglement**
   Two qubits are said to be entangled when their combined state cannot be factored into separate states for each qubit. For example, the entangled state of two qubits can be written as:

   $$|\psi_{entangled}\rangle = \frac{1}{\sqrt{2}}(|00\rangle + |11\rangle)$$

   - In this state, if one qubit is measured as `0`, the other qubit will also collapse to `0`. Similarly, if one qubit is measured as `1`, the other qubit will also collapse to `1`.
   - This correlation holds even if the qubits are separated by vast distances, a property experimentally confirmed and essential to technologies like quantum cryptography.
2. **Significance of Entanglement**
   - Entanglement allows qubits to share information in ways that classical systems cannot, enabling profound interdependencies across quantum states.
   - It facilitates phenomena like **quantum teleportation**, where the state of one qubit is transferred to another distant qubit without transmitting physical particles.
3. **Role in Quantum Computing**
   - Entanglement is critical for many quantum algorithms, such as Grover's search algorithm and Shor's factoring algorithm.
   - It enables **distributed quantum computing**, where entangled qubits across different systems collaborate to solve problems.

Quantum Parallelism: A Synergy of Superposition and Entanglement

The combined power of superposition and entanglement enables **quantum parallelism**, the ability of quantum computers to perform multiple calculations simultaneously.

1. **Superposition Enables Parallel Computation**
   - A single qubit in superposition can explore two possibilities (`0` and `1`) simultaneously.
   - An n-qubit system in superposition can encode 2^n possibilities at once, exponentially expanding the computational space.
2. **Entanglement Enhances Computational Power**
   - Entanglement introduces intricate correlations between qubits, allowing quantum computers to encode and manipulate complex relationships that classical computers cannot easily simulate.
   - These correlations enable highly efficient processing of problems where the relationships between variables are crucial, such as optimization problems and quantum simulations.
3. **Example: Solving Problems Efficiently**
   - Consider the problem of searching an unsorted database with N entries. Classical algorithms require $O(N)$ steps to find a solution, but quantum algorithms like Grover's use superposition and entanglement to achieve $O(\sqrt{N})$ complexity, significantly reducing computational time.

Applications of Superposition and Entanglement

1. **Cryptography**
   - Entangled qubits form the backbone of **quantum key distribution (QKD)** protocols like BB84, which offer theoretically unbreakable security by detecting eavesdropping.
2. **Optimization**
   - Quantum parallelism allows quantum computers to efficiently solve optimization problems in logistics, finance, and machine learning, where exploring all possibilities simultaneously is advantageous.
3. **Simulating Quantum Systems**

- Quantum computers leverage superposition and entanglement to simulate complex quantum systems, such as chemical reactions and materials science, that are beyond classical computational capabilities.

4. **Machine Learning**
   - Quantum algorithms utilize superposition and entanglement to process high-dimensional data sets, accelerating tasks like feature selection, clustering, and neural network training.

Challenges in Leveraging Superposition and Entanglement

Despite their immense potential, superposition and entanglement are delicate phenomena that face practical challenges:

1. **Decoherence**
   - Superposition and entanglement are highly sensitive to environmental disturbances, which can disrupt quantum states and lead to errors.
2. **Error Correction**
   - Quantum systems require robust error-correction mechanisms to maintain the integrity of superposition and entanglement.
3. **Scalability**
   - Building large-scale quantum systems with many entangled qubits is an ongoing challenge due to hardware limitations and error rates.

Quantum superposition and **quantum entanglement** are not just fascinating physical phenomena but foundational enablers of quantum computing. Superposition allows qubits to exist in multiple states simultaneously, exponentially expanding computational possibilities. Entanglement creates deep correlations between qubits, enabling the collaborative processing of information. Together, they empower **quantum parallelism**, allowing quantum computers to tackle problems of unprecedented complexity and scale.

These principles herald a paradigm shift in computation, offering profound opportunities across cryptography, optimization, scientific simulation, and beyond. While challenges remain, the continued exploration and application of superposition and entanglement are shaping the future of technology, pushing the boundaries of what is computationally possible.

Quantum Gates and Circuits

Quantum gates and circuits are the operational framework of quantum computing, analogous to logic gates and circuits in classical computing. However, unlike classical gates, which manipulate binary bits, quantum gates operate on **qubits** and leverage the unique principles of **superposition**, **entanglement**, and **interference**. This ability to manipulate quantum states with precision is what enables quantum computers to solve complex problems in ways that are beyond the reach of classical systems.

In this section, we will explore the fundamental quantum gates, their operations, and how they form the building blocks of **quantum circuits**, the computational pathways of quantum computers.

What Are Quantum Gates?

Quantum gates are mathematical operators that manipulate the state of one or more qubits. These gates are represented as unitary matrices, ensuring that the transformations they perform are reversible (a key requirement in quantum mechanics). Unlike classical gates, which perform deterministic operations like AND, OR, or NOT, quantum gates exploit quantum phenomena to perform transformations that are probabilistic and multi-dimensional.

1. **Key Characteristics of Quantum Gates**:
    - **Unitary Operations**: Quantum gates preserve the total probability of the quantum system (i.e., the sum of probabilities equals 1).
    - **Reversibility**: All quantum gates are inherently reversible due to their unitary nature, unlike classical gates such as AND or OR.
    - **Quantum Parallelism**: By operating on qubits in **superposition**, quantum gates simultaneously affect all possible states the qubit represents, enabling **quantum parallelism**.
2. **Notation and Representation**: Quantum gates are often represented using **quantum circuit diagrams**, where qubits are shown as horizontal lines, and gates are depicted as symbols acting on those lines.

Basic Quantum Gates and Their Functions

1. **Single-Qubit Gates**
   Single-qubit gates act on a single qubit and perform operations like rotation or flipping.
   - **Pauli-X Gate (NOT Gate)**:
     The Pauli-X gate flips the state of a qubit, analogous to the classical NOT gate.

     $$X|0\rangle = |1\rangle \quad \text{and} \quad X|1\rangle = |0\rangle$$

     Matrix Representation:

     $$X = \begin{bmatrix} 0 & 1 \\ 1 & 0 \end{bmatrix}$$

     Use Case: Flipping qubit states or initializing qubits.

   - **Hadamard Gate (H Gate)**:
     The Hadamard gate creates a **superposition** state by transforming a qubit from a basis state ($|0\rangle$ or $|1\rangle$) into an equal-weighted combination of $|0\rangle$ and $|1\rangle$.

     $$H|0\rangle = \frac{1}{\sqrt{2}}(|0\rangle + |1\rangle), H|1\rangle = \frac{1}{\sqrt{2}}(|0\rangle - |1\rangle)$$

     Matrix Representation:

     $$H = \frac{1}{\sqrt{2}}\begin{bmatrix} 1 & 1 \\ 1 & -1 \end{bmatrix}$$

     Use Case: Initiating quantum parallelism by placing qubits into superposition.

   - **Phase Gate (S Gate)**:
     The S gate introduces a phase shift of $\pi/2$ to the qubit's state.

$$S = \begin{bmatrix} 1 & 0 \\ 0 & i \end{bmatrix}$$

Use Case: Modifying the phase of quantum states in algorithms requiring interference patterns.

- **T Gate**:
  Similar to the S gate, but introduces a phase shift of $\pi/4$.

2. **Multi-Qubit Gates**
   Multi-qubit gates manipulate multiple qubits simultaneously and introduce **entanglement**, the correlation of quantum states across qubits.
   - **Controlled-NOT Gate (CNOT Gate)**:
     The CNOT gate flips the state of a target qubit only if the control qubit is in the $|1\rangle$ state. It is a fundamental gate for creating entanglement.
     Truth Table:
     - Input: $|00\rangle, |01\rangle, |10\rangle, |11\rangle$
     - Output: $|00\rangle, |01\rangle, |11\rangle, |10\rangle$

     Matrix Representation:

$$CNOT = \begin{bmatrix} 1 & 0 & 0 & 0 \\ 0 & 1 & 0 & 0 \\ 0 & 0 & 0 & 1 \\ 0 & 0 & 1 & 0 \end{bmatrix}$$

     Use Case: Generating entangled states like the Bell State:

$$|\psi\rangle = \frac{1}{\sqrt{2}}(|00\rangle + |11\rangle)$$

   - **Toffoli Gate (CCNOT Gate)**:
     A three-qubit gate where the target qubit is flipped only when both control qubits are in the $|1\rangle$ state.
     Use Case: Quantum error correction and certain quantum algorithms.

Quantum Circuits: Constructing Computation Pathways

A **quantum circuit** is a sequence of quantum gates applied to a set of qubits to perform a computation. These circuits are represented as diagrams, with qubits as horizontal lines and gates as symbols.

1. **Structure of a Quantum Circuit**:
   - **Input State Preparation**: Qubits are initialized in a known state, often $|0\rangle$.
   - **Gate Operations**: Quantum gates are applied in sequence or parallel to manipulate the qubits.
   - **Measurement**: At the end of the circuit, qubits are measured, collapsing their states to classical outcomes.
2. **Building a Simple Quantum Circuit**: Example: Creating a Bell State

   - $|\psi\rangle = \frac{1}{\sqrt{2}}(|00\rangle + |11\rangle)$:

     - Start with two qubits in the $|0\rangle$ state.
     - Apply a Hadamard gate to the first qubit to create superposition.
     - Use a CNOT gate with the first qubit as the control and the second as the target to entangle them.

   Circuit Diagram:

$$|0\rangle \xrightarrow{H} \xrightarrow{CNOT} Measure$$

Applications of Quantum Gates and Circuits

1. **Quantum Algorithms**:
   Quantum gates and circuits form the foundation of powerful quantum algorithms such as:
   - **Shor's Algorithm**: Factorizes large numbers exponentially faster than classical algorithms.
   - **Grover's Algorithm**: Searches unstructured databases in $O(\sqrt{N})$, a quadratic speedup.

2. **Quantum Cryptography**:
   Quantum circuits enable secure communication through protocols like **quantum key distribution (QKD)**.
3. **Quantum Simulation**:
   Complex quantum systems, such as molecular interactions, can be simulated using quantum circuits.
4. **Error Correction**:
   Quantum circuits implement error correction codes to protect quantum computations from decoherence and noise.

Challenges in Building Quantum Circuits

1. **Decoherence**: Quantum states are highly fragile and can lose coherence due to environmental noise.
2. **Gate Fidelity**: Imperfections in quantum gates lead to errors, requiring high-precision operations.
3. **Scalability**: As the number of qubits increases, the complexity of constructing and maintaining accurate quantum circuits grows exponentially.

Quantum gates and circuits represent the operational core of quantum computing. By manipulating qubits using gates like Pauli-X, Hadamard, and CNOT, quantum circuits perform complex computations that exploit the principles of **superposition**, **entanglement**, and **interference**. These tools not only differentiate quantum computing from its classical counterpart but also enable revolutionary advancements across cryptography, optimization, and quantum simulation. Mastering the design and operation of quantum circuits is pivotal to unlocking the full potential of quantum computing.

Quantum Computing in Practice: A Glimpse of Current Hardware

Quantum computing is no longer confined to theoretical physics or isolated laboratories. Companies like IBM, Google, Rigetti, and others have developed quantum processors that provide a tangible glimpse into the potential of quantum computation. These systems, however, remain in their infancy, grappling with both monumental challenges and transformative opportunities. In this section, we will explore the **state-of-the-art quantum**

hardware, its underlying principles, the technological hurdles to scalability, and the promising pathways toward realizing practical quantum computers.

Current State of Quantum Hardware

The hardware landscape of quantum computing is dynamic, with various platforms and architectures competing to establish themselves as the most scalable and practical approach. These platforms rely on different physical systems to represent and manipulate **qubits**, including superconducting circuits, trapped ions, photonic qubits, and more. Here are some of the leading quantum hardware systems:

---

1. IBM Q

IBM is one of the frontrunners in quantum computing, offering access to quantum systems through its **IBM Quantum Experience** platform. Its hardware is based on **superconducting qubits**, where quantum states are created and manipulated using electrical currents cooled to near absolute zero.

- **Key Features**:
    - **IBM Q System One**: A commercially available quantum computer housed in a glass cube, showcasing the company's commitment to integrating quantum systems into practical applications.
    - **Qiskit**: IBM's open-source quantum programming framework allows users to design, simulate, and execute quantum algorithms on real quantum processors.
    - Current systems include processors like the 127-qubit **Eagle** and the ambitious roadmap toward systems with **thousands of qubits** by 2030.
- **Challenges**:
    - Superconducting qubits are highly susceptible to **decoherence** (loss of quantum information due to environmental interactions).
    - Error rates during quantum gate operations remain a significant limitation.

---

2. Google Sycamore

Google achieved a major milestone in 2019 with its **Sycamore** processor, claiming to have demonstrated **quantum supremacy**. This was achieved by performing a computation in 200 seconds that would take the world's most powerful classical supercomputer thousands of years.

- **Key Features**:
  - The Sycamore processor consists of 54 superconducting qubits, designed to minimize crosstalk (unintended interactions between qubits).
  - The architecture emphasizes **high-fidelity gate operations** and low error rates for quantum gates.
  - Google's hardware focuses on benchmarking quantum advantage, particularly in solving highly specialized problems.
- **Challenges**:
  - While Sycamore demonstrated quantum supremacy, the computation performed had limited real-world applications. Scaling the architecture for general-purpose computing remains a significant hurdle.
  - Thermal noise and quantum error correction are ongoing areas of research.

---

3. Rigetti Computing

Rigetti is a pioneer in **hybrid quantum-classical computing**, where quantum processors are used in conjunction with classical systems to solve complex problems. Rigetti's systems are also based on superconducting qubits and are accessible through its **Quantum Cloud Services (QCS)**.

- **Key Features**:
  - Emphasis on **programmability** and integration with classical systems.
  - Rigetti's hardware focuses on mid-sized quantum processors, including its 80-qubit Aspen processor.
  - The company's **Forest Development Kit** simplifies quantum software development.
- **Challenges**:

- Rigetti's qubits face the same coherence and noise challenges as other superconducting architectures.
- Scaling the number of qubits while maintaining gate fidelity is an ongoing challenge.

Other Notable Quantum Hardware Platforms

1. **IonQ (Trapped Ions)**:
   - Trapped ion systems use charged particles (ions) suspended in electromagnetic fields as qubits. These systems offer **high coherence times** and **precise gate operations**.
   - IonQ's processors have been shown to achieve leading gate fidelity, but scalability is limited due to the physical complexity of controlling large numbers of ions.
2. **D-Wave (Quantum Annealing)**:
   - D-Wave specializes in **quantum annealing**, a subset of quantum computing designed for optimization problems.
   - While not a general-purpose quantum computer, D-Wave systems are practical for specific applications like logistics and scheduling.
3. **Photonic Quantum Computing**:
   - Companies like **PsiQuantum** and **Xanadu** are developing quantum computers based on **photons** (light particles) as qubits. Photonic systems promise room-temperature operation and resilience to decoherence, but they face challenges in creating scalable entanglement.

Challenges in Building Scalable Quantum Systems

Despite rapid progress, quantum hardware faces a series of technical and theoretical obstacles:

1. **Decoherence and Noise**:
   Qubits are inherently fragile, with quantum states quickly degrading due to interactions with their environment. Achieving long **coherence times** is critical for performing meaningful computations.

2. **Quantum Error Correction**:
   Error rates in quantum gates are still too high for reliable computation. Quantum error correction codes, such as **surface codes**, require many physical qubits to create a single **logical qubit**, significantly increasing hardware complexity.
3. **Qubit Connectivity**:
   Many quantum algorithms require entangling qubits that are physically distant on the chip. Limited connectivity introduces additional overhead in designing circuits.
4. **Cryogenic Cooling**:
   Superconducting and many other quantum systems require cooling to near absolute zero. Maintaining such extreme conditions adds significant infrastructure costs.
5. **Scalability**:
   Moving from tens to thousands (or millions) of qubits requires advances in fabrication, control electronics, and error correction protocols.
6. **Integration with Classical Systems**:
   Hybrid quantum-classical computing will likely dominate the early practical use cases. Efficiently integrating quantum processors into classical workflows remains an open challenge.

Opportunities and Advancements in Quantum Hardware

Despite the challenges, there are promising avenues of research and innovation that are paving the way for scalable quantum systems:

1. **Quantum Error Correction Advances**:
   New methods of error correction, such as **topological qubits** (e.g., Microsoft's Majorana-based approach), promise to reduce the overhead required for fault-tolerant computation.
2. **Neutral Atom Quantum Computing**:
   Startups like **QuEra** are exploring neutral atom systems, which offer highly scalable architectures by leveraging laser-based manipulation of atomic arrays.
3. **Quantum Hardware Co-Design**:
   Companies are increasingly designing hardware and software in tandem to optimize performance. For example, Google and IBM are aligning hardware advancements with quantum algorithms for specific use cases.

4. **Room-Temperature Quantum Systems**:
   Photonic and diamond-based qubit systems (such as those using nitrogen-vacancy centers) aim to eliminate the need for cryogenic cooling, reducing operational complexity.
5. **Quantum Advantage for Specialized Applications**:
   Even before general-purpose quantum computers are realized, hardware platforms are finding niches in fields like **quantum chemistry**, **finance**, and **cryptography**, where they can demonstrate real-world advantages over classical systems.

Conclusion

Quantum hardware is at the frontier of scientific and technological innovation. Platforms like IBM Q, Google Sycamore, and Rigetti are pushing the boundaries of what is possible, demonstrating proof-of-concept systems that hint at quantum computing's transformative potential. However, the road to scalable, fault-tolerant quantum computers is long and fraught with challenges, from decoherence and error correction to physical scalability and infrastructure requirements.

Despite these hurdles, the opportunities presented by quantum computing—ranging from solving intractable optimization problems to advancing materials science and cryptography—continue to inspire groundbreaking research and investment. The next decade promises to be a pivotal era as hardware systems evolve from experimental prototypes to practical tools, unlocking new possibilities across science, industry, and society.

CHAPTER 2: Basics of Machine Learning

DESCRIPTION:

This chapter provides an essential introduction to machine learning, focusing on key concepts, techniques, and workflows. Readers will learn about supervised and unsupervised learning, explore popular machine learning algorithms, and understand the role of frameworks like TensorFlow and PyTorch in building models. By bridging foundational concepts with practical examples, this chapter ensures readers have the necessary knowledge to integrate machine learning into quantum applications.

What is Machine Learning?

Machine learning (ML) is a transformative branch of artificial intelligence (AI) that enables computers to learn from data and make decisions or predictions without being explicitly programmed for specific tasks. At its core, machine learning is about finding patterns in data and using those patterns to perform tasks like classifying images, forecasting trends, or identifying anomalies. This ability to adapt and improve over time through experience makes machine learning a cornerstone of modern technology.

Definition and Purpose of Machine Learning

Definition: Machine learning is a subfield of AI that focuses on developing algorithms capable of learning and improving from experience. Unlike traditional programming, where explicit rules are coded to solve a problem, machine learning systems discover patterns and relationships in data to develop solutions.

Purpose: The primary goal of machine learning is to enable automation of complex, data-driven tasks. Its applications range from personalized recommendations (like in Netflix and Spotify) to advanced medical diagnostics, autonomous vehicles, and natural language processing (e.g., chatbots). By leveraging vast amounts of data, machine learning helps organizations make faster, smarter, and more accurate decisions.

Classical Programming vs. Machine Learning

The difference between classical programming and machine learning lies in **how solutions are generated**.

- **Classical Programming**:
  In classical programming, a developer writes explicit instructions or rules for a system to follow. These rules are manually coded and often work well for deterministic tasks like calculating taxes or managing inventory. The system processes inputs based on these hardcoded rules to generate outputs.
  Example: A calculator program explicitly follows rules (e.g., addition, subtraction).
- **Machine Learning**:
  In machine learning, instead of coding explicit rules, you provide a system with

data and an algorithm that learns patterns and relationships from the data. The system then generates its own logic (or model) to map inputs to outputs.
Example: In a facial recognition system, you feed the model thousands of images of faces, and the system learns to identify distinguishing features like eyes, noses, and facial contours.

Key Difference: Classical programming relies on fixed, pre-defined logic; machine learning builds flexible, data-driven models that adapt to new scenarios.

How Does Machine Learning Work?

At a high level, the process of machine learning involves the following steps:

1. **Data Collection**: Gathering relevant data that represents the problem you want to solve.
2. **Data Preparation**: Cleaning, transforming, and organizing the data into a format suitable for analysis.
3. **Model Selection**: Choosing a machine learning algorithm based on the task (e.g., classification, regression).
4. **Training**: Feeding the algorithm training data to develop a model by identifying patterns in the data.
5. **Testing and Validation**: Evaluating the model on unseen data to ensure accuracy and reliability.
6. **Deployment**: Using the trained model to make predictions or decisions in real-world scenarios.
7. **Iterative Improvement**: Continuously refining the model by adding more data or tweaking algorithms.

Why Is Machine Learning Important?

The significance of machine learning lies in its ability to process massive amounts of data, extract meaningful insights, and automate decision-making. Traditional programming is unable to handle the scale and complexity of many modern challenges, such as understanding human language, predicting customer behavior, or detecting subtle anomalies in financial systems. Machine learning overcomes these challenges by harnessing data-driven intelligence.

Key Benefits:

- **Scalability**: Can analyze large datasets far beyond human capability.
- **Adaptability**: Learns and evolves with new data, improving over time.
- **Precision**: Reduces human error and enhances decision-making accuracy.
- **Automation**: Reduces the need for manual intervention in repetitive, data-driven tasks.

Types of Machine Learning

Machine learning can be broadly categorized into three types:

1. **Supervised Learning**:
    - The algorithm is trained on labeled data (data with input-output pairs).
    - Goal: Predict the output for new, unseen inputs.
    - Examples: Spam email detection, stock price prediction.
2. **Unsupervised Learning**:
    - The algorithm works on unlabeled data, identifying patterns or structures within it.
    - Goal: Group similar items or detect anomalies.
    - Examples: Customer segmentation, fraud detection.
3. **Reinforcement Learning**:
    - The algorithm learns by interacting with its environment, receiving feedback (rewards or penalties) based on its actions.
    - Goal: Maximize long-term rewards.
    - Examples: Training robots to walk, game-playing AI like AlphaGo.

Real-World Applications of Machine Learning

Machine learning is deeply integrated into our daily lives:

- **Healthcare**: Diagnosing diseases, drug discovery, and personalized treatment plans.

- **Finance**: Fraud detection, algorithmic trading, and credit scoring.
- **Retail**: Personalized product recommendations, inventory management, and dynamic pricing.
- **Transportation**: Autonomous vehicles, traffic prediction, and route optimization.
- **Entertainment**: Content recommendation systems like Netflix or Spotify.
- **Natural Language Processing**: Chatbots, voice assistants, and language translation.

The Future of Machine Learning

The importance of machine learning will only grow as more industries adopt data-driven approaches. With advances in computing power, data availability, and algorithmic innovation, machine learning will continue to solve problems that were once thought unsolvable.

Emerging trends include:

- The convergence of **quantum computing and machine learning** to tackle even larger datasets and more complex models.
- Enhanced interpretability and ethical considerations to ensure fairness and transparency in ML applications.
- Real-time, edge-based machine learning that operates on devices with limited computational power.

By understanding the foundational principles of machine learning and its immense potential, you'll be equipped to explore its intersection with quantum computing in the chapters ahead.

Types of Machine Learning: Supervised, Unsupervised, and Reinforcement Learning

Machine learning (ML) is a diverse and expansive field with multiple paradigms tailored to specific types of problems and data. At its core, machine learning can be classified into three main paradigms: **supervised learning**, **unsupervised learning**, and **reinforcement learning**. Each of these approaches has unique methodologies, objectives, and real-world applications that distinguish them from one another.

Supervised Learning

Definition:
Supervised learning is a paradigm where a model is trained using labeled datasets. The term "labeled" means that the input data comes with corresponding output data (often referred to as ground truth). The model's objective is to learn a mapping from inputs to outputs so it can make accurate predictions on new, unseen data.

How It Works:

1. **Training Phase**: The model is presented with input-output pairs (e.g., feature variables and their corresponding target labels).
2. **Learning Process**: The model minimizes the error between its predicted outputs and the actual outputs by adjusting its internal parameters.
3. **Evaluation and Prediction**: Once trained, the model is tested on new inputs to predict outputs accurately.

Key Algorithms:

- Linear Regression
- Logistic Regression
- Decision Trees
- Support Vector Machines (SVMs)
- Neural Networks

Practical Use Cases:

- **Spam Email Detection**: Classifies emails as spam or not spam based on labeled examples.
- **Credit Scoring**: Predicts whether a borrower is likely to default on a loan using historical labeled data.
- **Image Classification**: Identifies objects in images (e.g., cat vs. dog) using labeled image datasets.
- **Fraud Detection**: Flags fraudulent transactions by learning from past fraudulent and non-fraudulent activities.

Unsupervised Learning

Definition:
Unsupervised learning deals with data that has no explicit labels or predefined outputs. The model's task is to uncover hidden patterns, structures, or relationships within the data. Instead of mapping inputs to outputs, unsupervised learning focuses on understanding the underlying data distribution.

How It Works:

1. **Input Data**: The model receives only input features without corresponding labels.
2. **Learning Process**: The algorithm attempts to group, cluster, or compress data based on inherent similarities or distributions.

Key Algorithms:

- K-Means Clustering
- Hierarchical Clustering
- Principal Component Analysis (PCA)
- Autoencoders

Practical Use Cases:

- **Customer Segmentation**: Grouping customers into clusters based on purchasing behavior for targeted marketing.
- **Anomaly Detection**: Identifying outliers in datasets, such as fraudulent activities or manufacturing defects.
- **Dimensionality Reduction**: Simplifying high-dimensional datasets while preserving critical information for visualization or model building.
- **Recommender Systems**: Suggesting products (e.g., Amazon, Netflix) by identifying patterns in user preferences.

Key Challenge:
Unlike supervised learning, unsupervised learning lacks clear ground truth, making it harder to evaluate the model's performance.

Reinforcement Learning

Definition:
Reinforcement learning (RL) is a paradigm where an agent learns to make decisions by interacting with its environment. The agent receives feedback in the form of rewards or penalties based on its actions and seeks to maximize cumulative rewards over time.

How It Works:

1. **Agent and Environment**: The agent observes the environment and takes actions to achieve a specific goal.
2. **Feedback Loop**: The agent receives rewards (positive feedback) or penalties (negative feedback) based on the quality of its actions.
3. **Learning Process**: Over multiple iterations, the agent refines its policy (a mapping from states to actions) to optimize long-term rewards.

Key Concepts:

- **State**: The current situation or configuration in the environment.
- **Action**: A decision made by the agent to affect the environment.
- **Reward**: Feedback indicating the success or failure of an action.
- **Policy**: The strategy used by the agent to decide actions based on states.
- **Value Function**: An estimate of the expected cumulative reward from a given state.

Key Algorithms:

- Q-Learning
- Deep Q-Networks (DQN)
- Policy Gradient Methods
- Actor-Critic Methods

Practical Use Cases:

- **Autonomous Vehicles**: Training self-driving cars to navigate and make decisions in real-world environments.
- **Game AI**: Developing agents that can beat human players in games like Chess, Go, or StarCraft (e.g., AlphaGo, OpenAI Five).

- **Robotics**: Teaching robots to perform tasks like walking, object manipulation, or assembly.
- **Dynamic Pricing**: Setting prices dynamically based on changing market conditions and user behavior.

Strengths:
Reinforcement learning excels in sequential decision-making tasks where the agent must balance short-term rewards with long-term objectives.

Comparison of the Three Paradigms

Aspect	Supervised Learning	Unsupervised Learning	Reinforcement Learning
Input Data	Labeled	Unlabeled	Feedback from environment
Output	Predictive (explicit labels)	Descriptive (hidden patterns)	Prescriptive (actions/policies)
Goal	Learn a mapping from input to output	Discover structure in data	Maximize long-term rewards
Common Applications	Classification, regression	Clustering, dimensionality reduction	Autonomous systems, game AI

Real-World Integration

While these paradigms are distinct, they can also work together to address complex problems:

1. **Preprocessing with Unsupervised Learning**: Clustering techniques can organize raw data, which can then be labeled and fed into supervised models.
2. **Combining Supervised and Reinforcement Learning**: In self-driving cars, supervised learning models identify objects like pedestrians, while reinforcement learning handles decision-making and control.

The Significance of Understanding Paradigms

Recognizing the differences between supervised, unsupervised, and reinforcement learning is crucial for applying machine learning effectively. Each paradigm is suited to specific problems, and selecting the right approach depends on factors like the availability of labeled data, the complexity of the task, and the feedback environment. Mastery of these paradigms forms the foundation for advancing into specialized fields such as **quantum machine learning**, where these techniques are adapted to exploit the capabilities of quantum computing.

Core Machine Learning Algorithms

Machine learning algorithms form the backbone of AI-powered decision-making, enabling computers to learn patterns from data and make predictions or classifications. Each algorithm has unique characteristics, assumptions, and applications, making them suitable for specific types of problems. In this section, we explore key algorithms in machine learning, including **linear regression**, **decision trees**, **support vector machines (SVMs)**, **k-means clustering**, and **neural networks**. Additionally, we discuss their inner workings, strengths, limitations, and practical use cases.

1. Linear Regression

Overview:
Linear regression is one of the simplest and most widely used supervised learning algorithms for regression tasks. It models the relationship between an independent variable (or variables) and a dependent variable by fitting a linear equation to the observed data.

Mathematical Model:
The relationship is expressed as:

$$\mathcal{Y} = \beta_0 + \beta_1 x_1 + \beta_2 x_2 + \cdots + \beta_n x_n + \epsilon$$

Where:

- $\mathcal{Y}$: Dependent variable (target)
- x_n: Independent variable (features)
- β_n: Coefficients (weights)

- ϵ: Error term

Key Characteristics:

- **Assumption**: The relationship between variables is linear.
- **Output**: Predicts continuous values (e.g., house prices, stock trends).

Applications:

- Forecasting sales or revenue trends.
- Estimating relationships between factors (e.g., age and income).
- Predicting continuous outcomes, like temperature or demand.

Strengths:

- Easy to interpret and implement.
- Works well for linearly separable data.

Limitations:

- Performs poorly on non-linear data unless feature engineering or transformation is applied.

---

2. Decision Trees

Overview:

Decision trees are versatile supervised learning algorithms used for both classification and regression tasks. They operate by splitting the dataset into smaller subsets based on feature values, creating a tree-like structure of decision rules.

How It Works:

1. The tree starts at a root node.
2. The dataset is split into subsets based on the feature that minimizes impurity (measured using criteria like Gini Index or entropy).
3. Splitting continues recursively until the tree reaches terminal nodes (leaves).

Key Characteristics:

- **Intuitive Representation**: Each path from the root to a leaf represents a decision rule.
- **Handles Categorical and Numerical Data**: Adaptable to diverse datasets.

Applications:

- Credit risk assessment.
- Medical diagnosis (e.g., decision trees to classify diseases).
- Predicting customer churn.

Strengths:

- Easy to visualize and explain to non-technical stakeholders.
- No need for extensive preprocessing.

Limitations:

- Prone to overfitting if not pruned or regularized.
- Can be unstable with small changes in data.

---

3. Support Vector Machines (SVMs)

Overview:
Support vector machines are powerful supervised learning algorithms used for classification and regression tasks. They aim to find the hyperplane that best separates data points into different classes while maximizing the margin (distance between the hyperplane and nearest data points).

Key Concepts:

- **Hyperplane**: A decision boundary that separates different classes in feature space.
- **Support Vectors**: Data points closest to the hyperplane that influence its position.
- **Kernel Trick**: Maps data into higher-dimensional spaces to handle non-linearly separable data.

Applications:

- Image classification (e.g., handwriting recognition).
- Detecting anomalies in datasets (e.g., fraud detection).
- Text classification (e.g., spam detection).

Strengths:

- Effective in high-dimensional spaces.
- Works well for both linear and non-linear problems (via kernels).

Limitations:

- Computationally expensive for large datasets.
- Choosing the right kernel and parameters requires expertise.

---

4. K-Means Clustering

Overview:
K-means clustering is an unsupervised learning algorithm used for partitioning a dataset into **k clusters**, where each cluster contains data points that are more similar to one another than to those in other clusters.

How It Works:

1. **Initialization**: Randomly select kkk centroids.
2. **Assignment Step**: Assign each data point to the nearest centroid.
3. **Update Step**: Recalculate the centroids by averaging the points in each cluster.
4. Repeat until convergence.

Key Characteristics:

- Requires defining *k*, the number of clusters, in advance.
- Sensitive to the initial choice of centroids.

Applications:

- Market segmentation (e.g., clustering customers by buying behavior).

- Image compression (e.g., reducing the number of colors in an image).
- Identifying patterns in unlabeled datasets.

Strengths:

- Simple and fast for small to medium-sized datasets.
- Works well for datasets with clearly defined clusters.

Limitations:

- Struggles with non-spherical or overlapping clusters.
- Sensitive to outliers and scaling of data.

---

5. Neural Networks

Overview:
Neural networks are a family of machine learning algorithms inspired by the structure and function of the human brain. They consist of interconnected layers of neurons that process input data and learn complex patterns through iterative adjustments of weights and biases.

Structure:

- **Input Layer**: Receives raw data (e.g., pixels, numerical features).
- **Hidden Layers**: Perform computations using activation functions (e.g., ReLU, Sigmoid).
- **Output Layer**: Produces final predictions or classifications.

Learning Process:

1. **Forward Propagation**: Data flows through the network, generating predictions.
2. **Loss Calculation**: Measures the error between predictions and actual values.
3. **Backpropagation**: Adjusts weights and biases to minimize loss using gradient descent.

Applications:

- Image recognition (e.g., detecting faces, objects, or scenes).
- Natural language processing (e.g., language translation, sentiment analysis).

- Autonomous systems (e.g., self-driving cars, robotics).

Strengths:

- Capable of capturing highly non-linear and complex patterns.
- Scalable to large datasets with high-dimensional data.

Limitations:

- Computationally intensive and requires significant data for effective training.
- Challenging to interpret and debug (often considered a "black box").

When to Apply Each Algorithm

Algorithm	Best For	Examples
Linear Regression	Predicting continuous outcomes; establishing linear relationships	Forecasting trends, price prediction
Decision Trees	Intuitive decision-making; handling categorical and numerical data	Medical diagnosis, customer segmentation
Support Vector Machines	Classification with complex boundaries; high-dimensional data	Spam detection, fraud detection
K-Means Clustering	Finding natural groupings in unlabeled data	Market segmentation, pattern recognition
Neural Networks	Tackling non-linear, large-scale problems with high-dimensional data	Image recognition, language translation

---

Real-World Integration

Machine learning is rarely confined to a single algorithm. Instead, the choice of algorithm depends on the problem at hand, the size and nature of the dataset, and the desired outcomes. Often, multiple algorithms are combined or tested (using techniques like cross-validation or ensemble methods) to determine the most effective solution. Mastery of these algorithms provides the foundation for advancing into deeper areas of machine learning, such as ensemble learning, transfer learning, and deep learning.

The Machine Learning Workflow: From Data to Deployment

Building a machine learning model is not merely about choosing the right algorithm—it is a systematic, multi-stage process that transforms raw data into actionable insights or predictions. Each stage of the machine learning workflow is critical, interdependent, and tailored to address specific aspects of the problem at hand. Below, we explore the workflow in detail, covering key phases such as **data collection, preprocessing, model training, evaluation, deployment, and beyond**. This comprehensive approach ensures the creation of robust, efficient, and scalable machine learning solutions.

---

1. Data Collection: Gathering the Foundation

Objective:
Acquire relevant, high-quality data to serve as the foundation of the machine learning process.

Key Considerations:

- **Data Sources**: Identify where data will come from, such as databases, APIs, web scraping, sensors, or user interactions.
- **Relevance**: Ensure the data aligns with the problem being solved. Irrelevant data can lead to poor model performance.
- **Volume and Variety**: Determine whether the dataset is large and diverse enough to represent the underlying problem space effectively.

Example:
For a recommendation system, data may include user demographics, past purchases, browsing history, and item metadata.

Challenges:

- Incomplete or missing data.
- Bias in data collection that could lead to unfair or inaccurate predictions.

---

2. Data Preprocessing: Cleaning and Transforming the Data

Objective:
Prepare raw data for use by the machine learning algorithm. This step ensures that the input is clean, consistent, and properly structured.

Key Steps:

- **Data Cleaning**: Remove missing values, outliers, or inconsistent entries.
- **Feature Selection**: Identify which features (variables) are most relevant to the problem.
- **Feature Engineering**: Transform raw data into a format that is more useful for the model, such as creating new features or normalizing data.
- **Scaling**: Standardize data to ensure uniform ranges (important for algorithms sensitive to scale, like SVMs and neural networks).
- **Splitting the Data**: Divide the dataset into training, validation, and testing sets (e.g., 70%-20%-10%) to evaluate performance fairly.

Example:
For a housing price prediction model, data preprocessing might include handling missing values for house sizes, encoding categorical variables like location, and scaling numerical features like price and square footage.

Challenges:

- Overengineering features that don't generalize to real-world data.
- Introducing noise or bias during preprocessing.

---

3. Model Training: Learning Patterns from Data

Objective:
Teach the machine learning model to identify patterns in the training data and minimize prediction errors.

Key Steps:

- **Algorithm Selection**: Choose an appropriate algorithm based on the problem type (e.g., linear regression for continuous outcomes, decision trees for classification).
- **Training**: Use the training dataset to adjust the model's parameters. This involves optimizing a loss function (e.g., Mean Squared Error for regression, Cross-Entropy Loss for classification).
- **Hyperparameter Tuning**: Fine-tune algorithm-specific parameters (e.g., learning rate, number of tree splits) to maximize performance.

Example:
Training a neural network to classify images involves feeding labeled data, calculating errors using backpropagation, and updating weights via gradient descent.

Challenges:

- Overfitting: When the model performs well on training data but poorly on unseen data.
- Underfitting: When the model fails to capture the complexity of the problem.

---

4. Model Evaluation: Measuring Performance

Objective:
Assess how well the trained model performs on unseen data to ensure its reliability and robustness.

Key Metrics:

- **Regression Problems**: Metrics like Mean Absolute Error (MAE), Mean Squared Error (MSE), and R^2.
- **Classification Problems**: Metrics like accuracy, precision, recall, F1-score, and ROC-AUC.
- **Cross-Validation**: Partition the training data into subsets (folds) to validate the model multiple times, reducing bias.

Steps in Evaluation:

1. Evaluate on the **validation set** during training to tune hyperparameters.
2. Use the **test set** after training to assess final performance.

Example:
A fraud detection system might measure success using recall (to minimize false negatives) and precision (to avoid flagging too many false positives).

Challenges:

- Imbalanced datasets can lead to misleading accuracy scores. For example, a model predicting all transactions as "non-fraud" may achieve high accuracy if fraud cases are rare.
- Over-reliance on a single metric may not capture the nuances of performance.

---

5. Model Deployment: Integrating into Real-World Applications

Objective:
Make the trained model accessible for real-world use, such as serving predictions to users or integrating it into existing systems.

Key Steps:

- **Deployment Platforms**: Deploy the model to platforms like cloud services (AWS, Azure, GCP), on-premise servers, or edge devices (smartphones, IoT).
- **APIs**: Expose the model as an API for seamless integration into applications.
- **Monitoring and Feedback**: Continuously monitor the model's performance in production and collect feedback to improve future iterations.

Example:
A chatbot powered by a natural language processing model could be deployed as a REST API that interacts with users via a website or messaging app.

Challenges:

- Handling scalability: Ensuring the model performs well under heavy user loads.
- Addressing drift: Real-world data may change over time, causing model accuracy to degrade (data drift).

---

6. Model Maintenance and Improvement

Objective:
Ensure that the model remains relevant and effective as new data becomes available and requirements evolve.

Key Steps:

- **Monitoring**: Track key metrics (e.g., accuracy, latency) to detect performance issues.
- **Retraining**: Periodically retrain the model using updated data to capture evolving trends.
- **Version Control**: Maintain multiple versions of the model to compare performance and ensure backward compatibility.

Example:
An e-commerce recommendation engine may need regular retraining to reflect seasonal changes, new product launches, or shifts in user preferences.

Challenges:

- Balancing between retraining frequency and system downtime.
- Managing user trust when model predictions evolve.

The Broader Context: Beyond the Basics

While the stages outlined above form the core machine learning workflow, there are additional considerations for building effective machine learning systems:

- **Explainability and Interpretability**: Especially for regulated industries (e.g., healthcare, finance), understanding why a model makes specific predictions is crucial.
- **Ethical AI**: Avoiding biases, ensuring fairness, and maintaining transparency in decision-making are integral to responsible AI development.
- **Cost Optimization**: Balancing computational resources and cloud infrastructure costs to maximize return on investment.

From Idea to Impact

The machine learning workflow is a structured journey from raw data to impactful solutions. Success hinges on mastering every stage, from meticulous data preprocessing to strategic deployment and iterative refinement. Each step is an opportunity to shape the model's performance, scalability, and usability in solving complex, real-world problems. Whether you're developing a predictive model for healthcare diagnostics or an AI assistant for personalized education, this workflow provides the roadmap to bridge the gap between theoretical algorithms and transformative applications.

Introduction to Popular ML Frameworks: TensorFlow and PyTorch

Machine learning frameworks like TensorFlow and PyTorch have revolutionized the field of artificial intelligence by providing developers, researchers, and practitioners with powerful tools to build, train, and deploy machine learning models. These frameworks abstract much of the complexity associated with implementing algorithms and optimizing them, enabling rapid experimentation and large-scale deployment. This section provides a foundational understanding of TensorFlow and PyTorch, highlighting their core features, key differences, and how to implement a simple machine learning model in both frameworks.

What Are TensorFlow and PyTorch?

TensorFlow

- **Developed By**: Google Brain Team (2015).
- **Primary Features**:
    - TensorFlow is a comprehensive open-source platform designed for machine learning and deep learning.
    - It supports computational graphs, enabling the visualization of complex model architectures.
    - Offers high-level APIs (like Keras) for rapid prototyping and lower-level APIs for custom development.
    - TensorFlow excels in production environments, with tools like TensorFlow Serving for model deployment.
    - Cross-platform capabilities allow it to run on CPUs, GPUs, and TPUs (Tensor Processing Units).

PyTorch

- **Developed By**: Facebook's AI Research (FAIR) team (2016).
- **Primary Features**:
  - PyTorch is a dynamic computational graph framework, meaning computations are defined and executed on the fly, offering greater flexibility for research and experimentation.
  - Its Pythonic nature makes it intuitive for Python developers.
  - PyTorch's eager execution simplifies debugging and integration with Python libraries.
  - Strong support for GPU acceleration and tools like TorchServe for model deployment.

Key Differences Between TensorFlow and PyTorch

Feature	TensorFlow	PyTorch
Computation Graphs	Static by default; uses `tf.function` for dynamic	Dynamic by default, enabling on-the-fly changes
Ease of Use	Slightly steeper learning curve	Intuitive and Pythonic
Deployment	Excellent production tools (e.g., TensorFlow Serving, TFLite)	TorchServe for deployment
Visualization	TensorBoard for built-in visualization	Integrates with third-party tools like Matplotlib
Popularity in Research	Widely used in production and applied ML	Dominates research due to flexibility

---

Building a Simple Machine Learning Model

To illustrate the practical use of these frameworks, let's implement a basic machine learning model that classifies data into two categories using a neural network. We'll use a simple dataset like the Iris dataset or synthetic data for binary classification.

Example in TensorFlow

Below is an example of a binary classifier using TensorFlow.

```
Python


import tensorflow as tf

from tensorflow.keras.models import Sequential

from tensorflow.keras.layers import Dense

from sklearn.datasets import make_classification

from sklearn.model_selection import train_test_split

from sklearn.preprocessing import StandardScaler


# Generate synthetic data

X, y = make_classification(n_samples=1000, n_features=10, n_classes=2,
random_state=42)

X_train, X_test, y_train, y_test = train_test_split(X, y, test_size=0.2,
random_state=42)


# Standardize the data

scaler = StandardScaler()

X_train = scaler.fit_transform(X_train)

X_test = scaler.transform(X_test)


# Build the TensorFlow model

model = Sequential([

    Dense(32, activation='relu', input_shape=(X_train.shape[1],)),
```

```
    Dense(16, activation='relu'),

    Dense(1, activation='sigmoid')  # Output layer for binary
classification

])


# Compile the model

model.compile(optimizer='adam', loss='binary_crossentropy',
metrics=['accuracy'])


# Train the model

model.fit(X_train, y_train, epochs=10, batch_size=32,
validation_split=0.2)


# Evaluate the model

loss, accuracy = model.evaluate(X_test, y_test)

print(f"Test Accuracy: {accuracy}")
```

Example in PyTorch

Now, let's implement the same model using PyTorch.

```
Python


import torch

import torch.nn as nn

import torch.optim as optim

from sklearn.datasets import make_classification

from sklearn.model_selection import train_test_split
```

```
from sklearn.preprocessing import StandardScaler

from torch.utils.data import DataLoader, TensorDataset


# Generate synthetic data

X, y = make_classification(n_samples=1000, n_features=10, n_classes=2,
random_state=42)

X_train, X_test, y_train, y_test = train_test_split(X, y, test_size=0.2,
random_state=42)


# Standardize the data

scaler = StandardScaler()

X_train = scaler.fit_transform(X_train)

X_test = scaler.transform(X_test)


# Convert data to PyTorch tensors

X_train_tensor = torch.tensor(X_train, dtype=torch.float32)

y_train_tensor = torch.tensor(y_train, dtype=torch.float32)

X_test_tensor = torch.tensor(X_test, dtype=torch.float32)

y_test_tensor = torch.tensor(y_test, dtype=torch.float32)


# Create DataLoader for batching

train_dataset = TensorDataset(X_train_tensor, y_train_tensor)

train_loader = DataLoader(train_dataset, batch_size=32, shuffle=True)


# Define the PyTorch model

class BinaryClassifier(nn.Module):

    def __init__(self, input_dim):
```

```
        super(BinaryClassifier, self).__init__()
        self.fc1 = nn.Linear(input_dim, 32)
        self.fc2 = nn.Linear(32, 16)
        self.fc3 = nn.Linear(16, 1)
        self.sigmoid = nn.Sigmoid()

    def forward(self, x):
        x = torch.relu(self.fc1(x))
        x = torch.relu(self.fc2(x))
        x = self.sigmoid(self.fc3(x))
        return x

model = BinaryClassifier(input_dim=X_train.shape[1])

# Define loss and optimizer
criterion = nn.BCELoss()  # Binary Cross Entropy Loss
optimizer = optim.Adam(model.parameters(), lr=0.001)

# Train the model
for epoch in range(10):
    for batch_X, batch_y in train_loader:
        outputs = model(batch_X).squeeze()
        loss = criterion(outputs, batch_y)
        optimizer.zero_grad()
        loss.backward()
        optimizer.step()
```

```
# Evaluate the model
with torch.no_grad():
    y_pred = model(X_test_tensor).squeeze()
    y_pred_classes = (y_pred > 0.5).float()
    accuracy = (y_pred_classes == y_test_tensor).float().mean()
    print(f"Test Accuracy: {accuracy.item()}")
```

Expanding Beyond Basics

Both TensorFlow and PyTorch offer advanced capabilities such as:

1. **Transfer Learning**: Use pre-trained models like ResNet, BERT, or GPT for specific tasks.
2. **Distributed Training**: Scale training across multiple GPUs or nodes.
3. **AutoML**: Automate the process of hyperparameter tuning and model architecture selection.
4. **Model Explainability**: Integrate tools like SHAP or LIME to understand model predictions.

Conclusion: Which Framework Should You Choose?

The choice between TensorFlow and PyTorch often depends on your goals:

- **For Research and Prototyping**: PyTorch's dynamic graph and Pythonic approach make it the go-to choice.
- **For Production and Scalability**: TensorFlow's ecosystem, including TensorFlow Lite and TensorFlow Serving, is ideal for large-scale deployment.

Mastering both frameworks equips you with the versatility to tackle a wide range of machine learning challenges, from research to real-world applications.

CHAPTER 3: Quantum Machine Learning: Bridge Two Worlds

DESCRIPTION:

This chapter introduces the emerging field of Quantum Machine Learning (QML), highlighting how quantum computing principles can enhance traditional machine learning techniques. Readers will explore the synergy between quantum mechanics and machine learning, learn about quantum data representations, and gain insight into the advantages and challenges of QML. This chapter bridges the gap between the foundational knowledge of Chapters 1 and 2, setting the stage for hands-on implementation in later chapters.

What is Quantum Machine Learning (QML)?

Quantum Machine Learning (QML) represents the convergence of two transformative fields: **quantum computing** and **machine learning**. At its core, QML leverages the principles of quantum mechanics—such as superposition, entanglement, and quantum parallelism—to enhance traditional machine learning algorithms. This integration opens up new possibilities for solving computational problems that are either infeasible or inefficient using classical computing methods.

Defining Quantum Machine Learning

Machine learning involves teaching computers to learn from data and make predictions or decisions without explicit programming for each task. Classical machine learning methods rely on classical computers, which process information in binary form (0s and 1s). In contrast, QML incorporates **quantum computing**, a paradigm that utilizes **qubits**—quantum counterparts to classical bits—which can exist in multiple states simultaneously.

This quantum advantage allows QML algorithms to process and analyze data in ways that classical algorithms cannot, particularly for problems involving large, complex datasets, high-dimensional spaces, or intricate optimization challenges.

Key Characteristics of QML

1. **Quantum Speedup**
   Quantum computing's ability to process multiple states simultaneously (via superposition) and its inherent parallelism can significantly speed up certain machine learning tasks. Algorithms like Grover's search or the Harrow-Hassidim-Lloyd (HHL) algorithm promise faster solutions for data processing and matrix inversion—key steps in many machine learning workflows.
2. **High-Dimensional Problem Solving**
   Quantum systems naturally operate in **Hilbert space**, which is exponentially larger than classical space. This enables QML to model and process high-dimensional datasets efficiently, making it particularly powerful for problems like feature selection, dimensionality reduction, and pattern recognition.

3. **Probabilistic Computing**
   Unlike deterministic classical computing, quantum mechanics is inherently probabilistic. QML algorithms embrace this nature, allowing for robust handling of uncertainty and noise in data, which are common in real-world machine learning scenarios.

Why Quantum Machine Learning Matters

The promise of QML lies in its **potential benefits** over classical machine learning:

1. **Efficiency Gains**
   Many machine learning tasks, such as training neural networks or performing optimization, involve significant computational costs. Quantum algorithms can reduce the time complexity of these tasks, enabling faster training and inference.
2. **Better Handling of Complex Data**
   Quantum computing can process **entangled datasets**, where relationships between data points are intricate and non-linear, in ways classical systems cannot. This is particularly useful for problems like natural language processing, image recognition, and bioinformatics.
3. **Enhanced Optimization**
   Many machine learning tasks, such as finding the best hyperparameters or minimizing loss functions, are optimization problems. Quantum optimization techniques can explore solution spaces more effectively, avoiding pitfalls like getting stuck in local minima.
4. **Scalability**
   As datasets grow larger and more complex, classical computing struggles with scalability. Quantum computing offers a potential pathway to manage these challenges, providing tools to analyze massive datasets with greater efficiency.

Applications of Quantum Machine Learning

1. **Finance**
   Quantum-enhanced algorithms can optimize portfolio management, fraud detection, and financial modeling with improved precision and speed.
2. **Healthcare**
   QML is poised to revolutionize drug discovery, genomic analysis, and personalized medicine by accelerating the analysis of complex biological data.
3. **Artificial Intelligence**
   Quantum systems can empower deep learning architectures, enabling advancements in AI applications such as natural language processing, autonomous vehicles, and recommendation systems.
4. **Logistics and Optimization**
   Industries like transportation and supply chain management can benefit from QML's ability to solve complex optimization problems, such as route planning and resource allocation, more efficiently.
5. **Cybersecurity**
   Quantum computing can improve encryption and threat detection by analyzing vast amounts of security data in real time.

Challenges in QML

While the potential of QML is vast, it is important to recognize the **current limitations** and **challenges** of the field:

1. **Hardware Constraints**
   Quantum hardware is still in its infancy. Issues such as qubit instability (decoherence) and error rates limit the scalability of quantum systems.
2. **Integration with Classical Systems**
   Most QML algorithms today are hybrid, requiring classical systems to preprocess data and handle certain computations. Seamless integration of classical and quantum systems remains a challenge.
3. **Algorithm Development**
   Quantum machine learning is a relatively new field, and many algorithms are still in

the experimental phase. Significant research is needed to develop robust, scalable algorithms.

4. **Data Input and Output**
   Efficiently encoding large datasets into quantum systems and extracting meaningful results remains a technical bottleneck.

The Future of QML

Despite the challenges, the future of QML is promising. Advances in quantum hardware, such as IBM Q, Google Sycamore, and Rigetti systems, are rapidly improving the stability and scalability of quantum computers. At the same time, frameworks like TensorFlow Quantum, Qiskit, PennyLane, and Amazon Braket are making QML accessible to researchers and developers worldwide.

In the coming years, QML is expected to play a pivotal role in tackling problems that classical machine learning cannot, enabling breakthroughs across industries and scientific disciplines.

QML is not just a technological leap—it is a paradigm shift in how we approach data, computation, and artificial intelligence. By blending the best of quantum mechanics and machine learning, we stand on the brink of a new era of innovation and discovery.

Quantum Data and Quantum Features

Quantum data and quantum features form the foundational layer of Quantum Machine Learning (QML), bridging the classical and quantum worlds. These concepts enable the encoding of classical information into quantum states and the extraction of useful patterns for quantum-based computation. Understanding these elements is key to harnessing the potential of quantum systems for machine learning tasks.

What is Quantum Data?

Quantum data refers to information that exists in a quantum mechanical form. Unlike classical data, which is represented as binary numbers (0s and 1s), quantum data is encoded in **quantum states**, leveraging the unique properties of **qubits** such as **superposition** and **entanglement**.

There are two primary types of quantum data:

1. **Naturally Quantum Data**
   Data originating from quantum systems, such as quantum chemistry, quantum physics simulations, or data from quantum sensors. This type of data inherently exists in quantum form.
2. **Classical Data Encoded into Quantum States**
   Classical data that is mapped into a quantum representation, enabling quantum algorithms to process it. For example, classical datasets like images, financial data, or genomic sequences can be transformed into quantum states for analysis.

Why Encode Data into Quantum States?

Encoding data into quantum states is essential for leveraging the computational power of quantum systems. This process enables the quantum computer to perform operations on data that exploit quantum parallelism and high-dimensional spaces (Hilbert spaces).

Key reasons to encode data into quantum states:

1. **Quantum Speedup**: Quantum systems can process encoded data exponentially faster for certain algorithms.
2. **Enhanced Feature Extraction**: Encoding data into quantum states allows for more efficient exploration of relationships in high-dimensional spaces.
3. **Access to Quantum Algorithms**: Many quantum machine learning algorithms (e.g., Quantum Kernel Estimation) rely on data being represented in a quantum format.

Methods for Encoding Classical Data into Quantum States

To leverage quantum computing, classical data must first be transformed into quantum representations. This transformation is known as **quantum encoding** or **data embedding**. Several encoding techniques are commonly used:

1. **Basis Encoding**
   Each classical data point is directly mapped to the computational basis states of

qubits. For example, a binary vector `[0, 1, 1]` could be encoded as the quantum state `|011⟩`.

2. **Amplitude Encoding**
   Classical data is encoded into the amplitudes of a quantum state. For instance, a normalized vector $[x_1, x_2, x_3, \ldots, x_n]$ can be represented as a quantum state:

   $$|\psi\rangle = x_1|0\rangle + x_2|1\rangle + x_3|2\rangle + \cdots + x_n|n\rangle$$

   This method is efficient for high-dimensional data but requires data normalization.

3. **Angle Encoding (or Phase Encoding)**
   Classical data values are encoded into the rotation angles of qubits. For example, a classical value `x` could be encoded as a quantum state using a rotation gate:

   $$|\psi\rangle + \cos(x)\,|0\rangle + \sin(x)\,|1\rangle$$

4. **Hybrid Encoding**
   Combines multiple encoding schemes to represent different types of data features. This is particularly useful for heterogeneous datasets.

Quantum Features and Feature Maps

Once data is encoded into quantum states, the next step is to extract **quantum features**—representations that exploit quantum mechanics for better pattern recognition and analysis. **Quantum feature maps** are mathematical transformations that project data into a quantum Hilbert space, where relationships between data points can be analyzed with higher fidelity than in classical space.

What are Quantum Feature Maps?

Quantum feature maps are transformations that encode classical data into a quantum state using a parameterized quantum circuit. These circuits create a new representation of the data in a **high-dimensional quantum Hilbert space**, allowing quantum algorithms to uncover complex relationships.

Mathematically, a quantum feature map can be represented as:

$$\phi(x) = U(x)|0\rangle$$

Where:

- x is the classical data point.
- $U(x)$ is a parameterized quantum circuit that transforms the data.
- $|0\rangle$ is the initial state of the qubit.

Benefits of Quantum Feature Maps

1. **Enhanced Nonlinear Mapping**
Quantum feature maps allow for highly complex, nonlinear transformations of data that are difficult to achieve with classical techniques.
2. **Kernel Methods in QML**
Quantum feature maps enable the use of quantum kernels, which measure the similarity between data points in a quantum Hilbert space. These quantum kernels can significantly outperform classical kernels in certain applications.
3. **Dimensionality Reduction**
By projecting data into a quantum space, quantum feature maps can make high-dimensional problems more computationally manageable.

Applications of Quantum Data and Features in QML

1. **Quantum Kernel Estimation**
Quantum kernels, enabled by feature maps, are used to enhance classification and clustering tasks by improving the separation of classes in the quantum feature space.
2. **Quantum Neural Networks**
Quantum feature maps serve as input layers to quantum neural networks, allowing the network to operate on complex, high-dimensional data.

3. **Anomaly Detection**
   Quantum features improve the detection of outliers by identifying subtle patterns in large datasets that may not be evident using classical methods.
4. **Reinforcement Learning**
   Quantum data encoding is used in quantum reinforcement learning to model complex environments and optimize decision-making processes.

Challenges in Quantum Data and Feature Engineering

1. **Data Encoding Costs**
   Efficiently encoding large datasets into quantum states is a major challenge due to hardware limitations and computational overhead.
2. **Noise and Decoherence**
   Quantum systems are sensitive to environmental noise, which can degrade the fidelity of encoded data and extracted features.
3. **Scalability**
   As datasets grow larger, the number of qubits required for accurate encoding increases, presenting hardware constraints.
4. **Interpretability**
   The high-dimensional nature of quantum feature spaces makes it difficult to interpret results, posing challenges for explainable AI.

The Future of Quantum Data and Features

As quantum hardware matures, the ability to encode and process quantum data will improve dramatically. Advancements in error correction, qubit stability, and hybrid quantum-classical frameworks will enable seamless integration of quantum data processing into machine learning pipelines. Quantum features are expected to become an integral part of high-performance machine learning systems, driving breakthroughs across fields like healthcare, finance, and artificial intelligence.

In the realm of Quantum Machine Learning, quantum data and feature engineering will serve as the cornerstone for building robust, scalable, and transformative models that go beyond the limitations of classical computation.

Quantum vs. Classical Machine Learning: A Comparative Perspective

As the fields of quantum computing and machine learning converge, Quantum Machine Learning (QML) emerges as a transformative approach, offering new possibilities for tackling problems that are computationally intensive or intractable with classical methods. Understanding the key differences between **classical machine learning (ML)** and **quantum machine learning (QML)** provides critical insight into when and why quantum algorithms can outperform classical ones, as well as the current limitations and opportunities in this domain.

Classical Machine Learning: A Snapshot

Classical machine learning operates within the framework of conventional computing, where data is represented as binary bits (0s and 1s), and computations are carried out using deterministic algorithms. Classical ML techniques leverage structured and unstructured data to learn patterns and make predictions, with powerful tools like **neural networks**, **decision trees**, and **support vector machines (SVMs)**.

Key features of classical ML:

1. **Representation**: Relies on classical data stored in binary format.
2. **Algorithms**: Employs methods such as gradient descent, matrix algebra, and stochastic optimization.
3. **Hardware**: Runs on CPUs, GPUs, and increasingly specialized hardware like TPUs (Tensor Processing Units).
4. **Applications**: Widely used in image recognition, natural language processing, recommendation systems, and more.

While classical ML has achieved remarkable success, it faces limitations when dealing with:

- High-dimensional data spaces.
- Problems requiring exponential computational resources.

- Complex optimization landscapes.

Quantum Machine Learning: A New Paradigm

Quantum Machine Learning blends quantum computing with machine learning principles to exploit the unique properties of quantum mechanics—**superposition**, **entanglement**, and **quantum interference**. By leveraging these properties, QML algorithms operate in high-dimensional quantum spaces (Hilbert spaces) and achieve computational efficiencies unattainable by classical systems.

Key features of QML:

1. **Representation**: Encodes data into quantum states, enabling access to exponentially large feature spaces.
2. **Algorithms**: Utilizes quantum algorithms like the **Quantum Approximate Optimization Algorithm (QAOA)**, **Variational Quantum Circuits (VQC)**, and **Quantum Kernels**.
3. **Hardware**: Operates on quantum processors such as those developed by IBM, Google, and Rigetti.
4. **Applications**: Promising for quantum chemistry, portfolio optimization, cryptography, and natural sciences.

Core Differences: Classical vs. Quantum ML

Aspect	Classical ML	Quantum ML
Data Representation	Binary bits (0s and 1s)	Quantum states ((
Feature Space	Finite-dimensional vector spaces	Exponentially large Hilbert spaces.
Speed	Limited by classical computational constraints	Exploits quantum parallelism for potential speedup.
Algorithms	Classical optimization (e.g., gradient descent)	Quantum algorithms (e.g., QAOA, Grover's algorithm).

Noise Sensitivity	Low; deterministic hardware	High; quantum systems are sensitive to decoherence.
Hardware	CPUs, GPUs, TPUs	Qubits; quantum hardware still in development.
Applications	General-purpose ML tasks	Specialized problems requiring exponential resources.

Problems Where Quantum Algorithms Offer Advantages

Quantum algorithms hold promise for solving problems that are computationally expensive or fundamentally limited by classical approaches. Some key examples include:

1. **High-Dimensional Data**
   Quantum systems can naturally represent and manipulate high-dimensional data through their ability to encode information into quantum states. This is particularly advantageous for tasks like kernel-based classification and clustering.
2. **Optimization Problems**
   Many machine learning problems involve finding optimal solutions in large and complex search spaces. Quantum algorithms such as **QAOA** and **Quantum Annealing** can provide faster convergence to global optima compared to classical heuristics.
3. **Matrix Operations**
   Quantum computers excel at certain linear algebra tasks, such as solving systems of linear equations, which are core to many ML algorithms. For instance, the **Harrow-Hassidim-Lloyd (HHL)** algorithm offers exponential speedup in solving linear equations.
4. **Quantum Feature Mapping**
   Quantum feature maps enable the encoding of classical data into high-dimensional quantum spaces, allowing for enhanced pattern recognition and separation in tasks like support vector machines and kernel methods.
5. **Data Sampling**
   Quantum systems can efficiently sample from complex probability distributions,

which is valuable for generative models and probabilistic inference in machine learning.

6. **Quantum Neural Networks**
   QML provides novel architectures for quantum neural networks, leveraging the exponential capacity of quantum states to model complex data distributions.

Quantum Parallelism and Quantum Speedup

The defining advantage of QML lies in **quantum parallelism**, the ability of quantum systems to process multiple possibilities simultaneously. This enables quantum algorithms to:

1. Explore large search spaces in fewer steps (e.g., Grover's algorithm for unstructured search).
2. Perform operations on exponentially large quantum states with fewer physical resources.

While quantum speedup is problem-specific and does not apply universally, quantum systems demonstrate the potential for exponential or quadratic improvements in certain ML tasks.

Challenges and Current Limitations of QML

Despite its promise, QML is still in its infancy, facing several challenges:

1. **Hardware Limitations**: Quantum computers are currently noisy and have limited qubits, constraining the size and complexity of problems they can handle.
2. **Data Encoding Overhead**: Transforming classical data into quantum states (quantum encoding) can be computationally expensive.
3. **Algorithm Development**: Many quantum algorithms are still theoretical or require hybrid quantum-classical approaches to be practical.
4. **Decoherence**: Quantum systems are highly sensitive to environmental noise, leading to errors and loss of information.
5. **Scalability**: Scaling quantum hardware and algorithms for real-world applications remains a significant technical hurdle.

The Future of QML: Bridging the Gap

As quantum hardware advances, the integration of quantum and classical machine learning will deepen, unlocking new capabilities. Some emerging trends include:

- **Hybrid Quantum-Classical Algorithms**: Leveraging the strengths of both quantum and classical systems, hybrid approaches like **Variational Quantum Circuits (VQC)** are becoming a practical pathway for implementing QML.
- **Error Correction**: Progress in quantum error correction will improve the reliability of quantum computations.
- **Domain-Specific Applications**: QML is expected to make breakthroughs in fields like drug discovery, financial modeling, and logistics optimization.

While classical machine learning remains the workhorse of modern AI, quantum machine learning represents the frontier of computational innovation. By combining the principles of quantum mechanics with machine learning, QML has the potential to solve problems previously considered intractable. Understanding the complementary roles of classical and quantum approaches will be crucial as we transition into the era of quantum-enhanced intelligence, where the synergy between the two will redefine the boundaries of what machines can learn and accomplish.

Hybrid Quantum-Classical Models: Merging the Power of Two Paradigms

As quantum computing continues to evolve, one of the most promising approaches to leveraging its power lies in hybrid quantum-classical models. These models combine the computational strengths of classical systems with the unique properties of quantum circuits to tackle problems that neither paradigm can efficiently solve alone. By understanding hybrid models, their architectures, and their practical applications, we unlock a pathway to harness the capabilities of quantum systems even in their nascent state, while retaining the reliability and scalability of classical systems.

What Are Hybrid Quantum-Classical Models?

A hybrid quantum-classical model is a computational framework where **classical computing resources** and **quantum processors** work in tandem. In these models:

1. Classical systems handle tasks that are well-suited to traditional computation, such as pre-processing data, gradient computations, and large-scale storage.
2. Quantum processors (quantum processing units, or QPUs) are used to perform quantum-specific tasks, such as sampling from complex distributions, performing quantum-enhanced optimizations, or encoding data into high-dimensional quantum spaces.

This synergy is particularly valuable because:

- **Quantum hardware is still limited** in terms of qubits and coherence times.
- Classical systems provide the infrastructure and stability needed to support quantum workloads.
- Combining the two allows us to solve practical problems today, even with noisy intermediate-scale quantum (NISQ) devices.

Core Principles of Hybrid Models

1. Variational Quantum Circuits (VQC)

Variational quantum circuits are at the heart of hybrid models. These circuits are parameterized quantum circuits designed to solve optimization problems by iteratively updating their parameters. A VQC workflow involves:

- Initializing a quantum circuit with adjustable parameters (e.g., rotation angles on qubits).
- Processing input data through the quantum circuit.
- Measuring the quantum output.
- Using a classical optimizer (e.g., gradient descent) to adjust the parameters based on the measurement results.

This iterative loop between quantum and classical systems allows the model to learn optimal parameters for specific tasks, such as classification, clustering, or regression.

---

2. Data Encoding into Quantum Circuits

Hybrid models begin by encoding classical data into quantum states, a process known as **quantum embedding** or **quantum feature mapping**. Techniques for data encoding include:

- **Amplitude encoding**: Encodes data into the amplitudes of quantum states.
- **Basis encoding**: Maps data into the computational basis states of qubits.
- **Angle encoding**: Represents data as rotation angles applied to qubits.

The choice of encoding determines the structure and richness of the feature space that the quantum circuit can explore.

---

3. Classical Optimization for Quantum Parameters

While quantum processors execute operations on qubits, classical systems perform essential optimization tasks. For instance:

- Loss functions (e.g., mean squared error or cross-entropy) are computed classically.
- Gradients of quantum parameters are evaluated using methods like the **parameter-shift rule**.
- Classical optimizers (e.g., Adam, RMSprop) update the quantum circuit parameters iteratively.

This hybrid feedback loop ensures efficient convergence even when quantum hardware is noisy or resource-limited.

Applications of Hybrid Models

1. Quantum Neural Networks (QNNs)

Hybrid quantum-classical models can extend the architecture of classical neural networks by integrating quantum circuits. A typical **Quantum Neural Network (QNN)** consists of:

- **Classical layers**: Perform traditional matrix operations, like weight multiplication and activation functions.

- **Quantum layers**: Use quantum circuits to capture complex relationships in data.

QNNs have shown promise in:

- **Pattern recognition**: Enhancing feature extraction in high-dimensional spaces.
- **Generative models**: Creating complex probability distributions for data generation.

2. Quantum Variational Autoencoders (QVAE)

Variational autoencoders (VAEs) are generative models that learn latent representations of data. In hybrid models:

- Classical components encode input data into latent variables.
- Quantum circuits perform optimization on these variables, enabling exploration of larger, richer latent spaces.

Applications of QVAEs include anomaly detection, image generation, and data compression.

3. Quantum-Assisted Optimization

Many real-world problems involve optimization challenges, such as portfolio allocation, supply chain management, and energy grid optimization. Hybrid models leverage quantum processors to solve subproblems within larger classical frameworks. For example:

- Quantum algorithms like the **Quantum Approximate Optimization Algorithm (QAOA)** can find near-optimal solutions for combinatorial optimization problems.
- Classical systems refine the solutions and integrate them into the broader workflow.

4. Reinforcement Learning

In reinforcement learning, agents learn to make decisions by maximizing rewards in an environment. Hybrid models use quantum circuits to enhance exploration of the solution space. For example:

- Quantum circuits can optimize the policy network in reinforcement learning.
- Classical systems handle simulation of the environment and reward computation.

Architectures of Hybrid Models

1. Fully-Integrated Models

In fully-integrated architectures, quantum circuits are embedded directly into the workflow of a classical model. For example:

- A classical neural network might include a quantum layer as part of its architecture.
- Data flows seamlessly between classical and quantum components during both training and inference.

2. Modular Architectures

In modular architectures, quantum and classical systems perform distinct tasks and communicate results intermittently. For instance:

- A quantum processor might handle feature extraction, while a classical system performs the final classification.
- Modular designs are particularly useful when quantum hardware is only capable of solving specific subproblems.

3. Alternating Architectures

In alternating architectures, the computation alternates between classical and quantum systems in an iterative loop. This is common in applications like variational quantum algorithms, where each iteration involves:

1. Classical computation of gradients.
2. Quantum updates to circuit parameters.

Advantages of Hybrid Models

1. **Overcoming Quantum Hardware Limitations**
   By delegating resource-intensive tasks to classical systems, hybrid models allow us to use today's noisy quantum devices effectively.

2. **Efficient Use of Quantum Resources**
   Hybrid models focus quantum resources on tasks where they provide the most significant advantage, such as high-dimensional feature extraction or optimization.
3. **Scalability**
   Classical systems provide the scalability needed for large datasets and complex workflows, while quantum systems enhance specific aspects of the computation.
4. **Flexibility**
   Hybrid architectures can be adapted to various applications, from machine learning to optimization and beyond.

Challenges of Hybrid Models

1. **Data Encoding Overhead**
   Encoding classical data into quantum states can be computationally expensive, reducing the overall speedup.
2. **Noisy Hardware**
   Current quantum devices suffer from decoherence and gate errors, which can introduce noise into hybrid computations.
3. **Algorithm Complexity**
   Designing hybrid algorithms that effectively leverage both quantum and classical resources is a complex task requiring expertise in both domains.
4. **Integration Bottlenecks**
   Efficient communication between quantum and classical systems is a technical challenge, particularly as quantum processors become more powerful.

Future of Hybrid Quantum-Classical Models

The development of hybrid models represents a crucial step toward practical quantum computing. As quantum hardware improves, hybrid architectures are expected to:

- Scale to larger problems and datasets.
- Enable real-time quantum-assisted decision-making.

- Drive advancements in fields like drug discovery, materials science, and artificial intelligence.

Moreover, hybrid models are laying the foundation for fully quantum workflows, where quantum systems will eventually handle end-to-end computations without relying on classical processors.

Hybrid quantum-classical models are a powerful bridge between today's classical machine learning capabilities and the quantum-driven future. By combining the strengths of both paradigms, these models enable us to explore quantum-enhanced solutions to complex problems while remaining grounded in the practical realities of classical computation. As the field advances, hybrid models will continue to unlock new possibilities, transforming industries and redefining the limits of computation.

Challenges and Future of Quantum Machine Learning (QML): Navigating the Road Ahead

Quantum Machine Learning (QML) is at the frontier of technological innovation, aiming to leverage the unique capabilities of quantum computing to revolutionize data processing and decision-making. However, this ambitious field faces numerous challenges, from hardware constraints to algorithmic complexities, that must be addressed before its full potential can be realized. At the same time, ongoing research and development are uncovering opportunities for groundbreaking advancements that could redefine the future of machine learning.

Challenges in Quantum Machine Learning

Despite its promise, QML is constrained by significant technical, practical, and theoretical challenges. These challenges span the entire workflow, from data preparation to algorithm design and deployment.

1. Hardware Limitations

Quantum computing hardware is still in its infancy, falling under the category of **Noisy Intermediate-Scale Quantum (NISQ)** devices. These systems face critical issues such as:

- **Limited Qubit Count**: Current quantum computers have relatively few qubits, restricting the size and complexity of problems they can tackle.
- **Error Rates and Decoherence**: Qubits are highly sensitive to noise and environmental interference, leading to short coherence times and unreliable results during lengthy computations.
- **Gate Fidelity and Connectivity**: Quantum gates (operations on qubits) are prone to errors, and not all qubits in a system are directly connected, which complicates algorithm design.

The consequence is that only small-scale or heavily simplified versions of quantum machine learning models can currently be implemented.

---

2. Data Encoding Complexity

One of the unique challenges of QML is **encoding classical data into quantum states**, a process that serves as the foundation for quantum computation. This step, while theoretically powerful, presents several difficulties:

- **Time Complexity**: Mapping large datasets into quantum states often requires exponential resources, eroding potential quantum speedups.
- **Encoding Fidelity**: Ensuring that the encoded quantum states accurately represent the original data is challenging, particularly for high-dimensional or noisy datasets.
- **Scalability**: The overhead of preparing data for quantum systems can diminish the computational advantage of QML in real-world scenarios.

---

3. Algorithmic Challenges

The design and implementation of quantum algorithms for machine learning introduce their own set of obstacles:

- **Algorithm Maturity**: Many QML algorithms, such as the Quantum Support Vector Machine (QSVM) or Variational Quantum Algorithms (VQA), are still in the experimental phase, lacking rigorous benchmarks against classical counterparts.
- **Gradient Vanishing in Quantum Circuits**: Training parameterized quantum circuits often suffers from vanishing gradients (barren plateaus), making optimization difficult.

- **Hybrid Integration**: Hybrid quantum-classical models, while promising, require seamless integration between quantum and classical systems—a non-trivial task given the differences in computation paradigms.

---

4. Scalability and Generalization

For QML to achieve widespread adoption, it must demonstrate scalability and generalization across diverse applications:

- **Model Scalability**: Expanding QML models to handle large datasets and complex tasks is currently hindered by hardware and algorithmic limitations.
- **Generalization Challenges**: QML models must prove their ability to generalize well across unseen data, particularly when applied to noisy or real-world datasets.

---

5. Resource Requirements

- **Quantum Resources**: Efficient QML algorithms often require an unrealistic number of qubits or error-corrected quantum systems, which are unavailable today.
- **Classical Support**: Hybrid models, which rely on classical systems for optimization, create computational bottlenecks that can negate the quantum advantage.

---

6. Talent and Interdisciplinary Expertise

The field of QML requires expertise in both quantum mechanics and machine learning—a combination of skills that is rare. Bridging the gap between physicists, computer scientists, and machine learning engineers is crucial for driving the field forward.

Future Directions and Opportunities in Quantum Machine Learning

While challenges persist, the future of QML is bright, with opportunities for groundbreaking advancements that could transform industries and redefine computing paradigms.

---

1. Advancements in Quantum Hardware

The continuous development of quantum hardware is a key driver of QML's future:

- **Error-Corrected Quantum Computers**: Ongoing research in error correction will lead to fault-tolerant quantum systems capable of running deep and accurate QML models.
- **Increased Qubit Counts**: As the number of qubits grows, larger and more complex QML models can be implemented, making them competitive with classical approaches.
- **Quantum Hardware Innovation**: Advances in superconducting qubits, trapped ions, and photonic quantum systems may yield faster, more stable, and scalable quantum processors.

---

2. Quantum Data and Applications

QML's potential lies in its ability to process **quantum-native data** that classical systems struggle to handle:

- **Quantum Chemistry and Materials Science**: Simulating molecular interactions and discovering new materials.
- **Optimization Problems**: Solving combinatorial optimization tasks in logistics, finance, and supply chain management.
- **High-Dimensional Feature Spaces**: Leveraging quantum feature maps for tasks like image classification and natural language processing.

By focusing on problems with inherently quantum properties, QML can showcase its advantages over classical machine learning.

---

3. Development of New Algorithms

Theoretical and algorithmic research will play a crucial role in expanding QML capabilities:

- **Hybrid Quantum-Classical Architectures**: Further development of hybrid models will enable practical applications using NISQ devices.
- **Quantum Neural Networks (QNNs)**: Advancements in QNN architectures may lead to highly expressive models for tasks such as generative modeling, clustering, and prediction.
- **Quantum Speedups**: Research into quantum algorithms that provide provable speedups over classical methods will solidify QML's relevance in the machine learning landscape.

---

4. Improved Data Encoding Techniques

To address the bottleneck of data encoding, researchers are exploring:

- **Efficient Embedding Methods**: Developing algorithms that map classical data into quantum states with minimal overhead.
- **Quantum Feature Engineering**: Designing quantum-specific features that enhance model performance and reduce encoding complexity.
- **Adaptive Encoding**: Creating dynamic encoding methods tailored to specific datasets and tasks.

---

5. Scalability Through Distributed Quantum Systems

Distributed quantum computing, where multiple quantum devices work together, may offer a solution to the scalability challenge. By parallelizing computations across quantum processors, researchers can overcome current hardware limitations.

---

6. Integration with Emerging Technologies

The intersection of QML with other cutting-edge fields will unlock new possibilities:

- **Artificial Intelligence**: Combining QML with advanced AI techniques for tasks like unsupervised learning and reinforcement learning.
- **Edge Computing**: Deploying QML models on edge quantum devices for real-time data processing in IoT and autonomous systems.
- **Cloud-Based Quantum Services**: Leveraging quantum cloud platforms (e.g., IBM Quantum, AWS Braket) for scalable and accessible QML experimentation.

---

7. Education and Workforce Development

As QML matures, education will play a pivotal role in addressing the talent gap:

- **Interdisciplinary Training Programs**: Courses that integrate quantum physics, computer science, and machine learning.
- **Open-Source Tools**: Platforms like TensorFlow Quantum and PennyLane will democratize QML development, making it accessible to a wider audience.

---

8. Ethical and Societal Considerations

As with any disruptive technology, QML must address ethical and societal implications:

- **Bias in Quantum Models**: Ensuring fairness and transparency in quantum-enhanced decision-making systems.
- **Data Privacy**: Balancing the power of QML with compliance to privacy regulations like GDPR and HIPAA.
- **Environmental Impact**: Mitigating the energy demands of large-scale quantum systems.

Quantum Machine Learning stands at the convergence of quantum computing and artificial intelligence, offering unprecedented opportunities to tackle some of the most complex problems in science and industry. While significant challenges remain—spanning hardware, algorithms, scalability, and expertise—ongoing advancements are poised to transform QML from a nascent field into a cornerstone of future computation. By addressing these challenges and capitalizing on emerging opportunities, QML has the potential to redefine how we understand and interact with data, opening doors to innovations that were once considered beyond reach.

PART 2: Mastering Quantum Machine Learning Frameworks

Part 2: Mastering Quantum Machine Learning Frameworks provides readers with hands-on experience using the most prominent tools and platforms for quantum machine learning. This section dives into practical implementation, starting with **TensorFlow Quantum (TFQ)** for building hybrid quantum-classical models, followed by **Qiskit**, IBM's robust framework for developing and simulating quantum circuits. Readers will then explore **PennyLane**, a versatile library for quantum differentiable programming, enabling seamless integration of quantum algorithms with machine learning workflows. Finally, the section covers **Amazon Braket**, a cloud-based platform that allows users to experiment with quantum machine learning models on real and simulated quantum hardware. By the end of this part, readers will have a comprehensive understanding of how to leverage these frameworks to design, test, and optimize quantum machine learning algorithms effectively.

CHAPTER 4: TensorFlow Quantum (TFQ)

DESCRIPTION:

This chapter dives into **TensorFlow Quantum (TFQ)**, a powerful library developed by Google for building and training quantum machine learning models. Readers will learn how TFQ integrates quantum circuits with classical machine learning frameworks, enabling hybrid quantum-classical workflows. The chapter covers installing TFQ, constructing quantum circuits, and applying quantum-enhanced models to practical problems using TensorFlow.

Introduction to TensorFlow Quantum

TensorFlow Quantum (TFQ) represents a groundbreaking evolution in the field of machine learning, combining the immense computational power of quantum computing with the robust and widely adopted TensorFlow ecosystem. As an open-source library developed by Google in collaboration with research partners, TensorFlow Quantum is specifically designed to accelerate quantum machine learning (QML) research by enabling seamless integration between quantum computations and classical machine learning workflows.

This introduction explores the purpose, architecture, and potential of TensorFlow Quantum, offering a detailed look at how this framework opens new possibilities for tackling problems that are computationally infeasible for classical systems.

What is TensorFlow Quantum?

TensorFlow Quantum is a specialized library that extends the TensorFlow framework to include quantum computations. It enables researchers and practitioners to define and manipulate quantum circuits as part of a larger machine learning pipeline, facilitating hybrid quantum-classical modeling. TFQ is particularly suited for variational quantum algorithms, quantum data encoding, and the study of quantum neural networks.

At its core, TensorFlow Quantum provides tools to:

- **Simulate Quantum Circuits**: Build and execute quantum circuits using classical simulators.
- **Integrate with Classical Models**: Combine quantum components with TensorFlow's existing machine learning tools to create hybrid models.
- **Optimize Quantum Algorithms**: Leverage TensorFlow's gradient-based optimization to train quantum machine learning models efficiently.

Purpose of TensorFlow Quantum

The primary purpose of TensorFlow Quantum is to simplify and streamline the process of developing quantum machine learning models. By embedding quantum operations within the familiar TensorFlow framework, TFQ empowers researchers to:

1. **Prototype Quantum Algorithms**: Quickly design and test quantum models without requiring direct access to quantum hardware.
2. **Bridge Quantum and Classical Worlds**: Enable hybrid solutions where quantum circuits complement classical machine learning models.
3. **Advance Quantum ML Research**: Provide a standardized platform for academic and industrial research in QML, lowering the barrier to entry for quantum computing.

TensorFlow Quantum is particularly significant in applications where classical machine learning struggles, such as:

- Solving combinatorial optimization problems.
- Understanding quantum systems.
- Exploring large-scale, high-dimensional datasets with quantum speedups.

Integration of Quantum Computing into TensorFlow's Ecosystem

TensorFlow Quantum is built on TensorFlow's foundation, making it an accessible tool for existing TensorFlow users. Here's how TFQ integrates quantum computing into the TensorFlow ecosystem:

1. **Quantum Circuit Representation**:
   TFQ introduces data structures for representing quantum circuits and quantum datasets within TensorFlow workflows. Circuits are built using Python-based tools like Cirq, an open-source quantum computing library developed by Google.
2. **Quantum Layers and Models**:
   Just as TensorFlow defines neural network layers, TFQ provides quantum circuit layers. These layers can be added to classical models to create hybrid quantum-classical architectures.
3. **Gradient-Based Optimization**:
   TensorFlow's automatic differentiation capabilities extend to quantum operations, allowing seamless optimization of quantum parameters in variational quantum algorithms.
4. **Quantum Simulators**:
   TFQ integrates with quantum simulators like Cirq's simulators, enabling users to

test quantum circuits on classical hardware before running them on actual quantum devices.

5. **Interoperability with TensorFlow Tools**:
   TFQ leverages TensorFlow's existing libraries, such as TensorFlow Extended (TFX) for deployment, TensorBoard for visualization, and Keras for rapid prototyping.

How TensorFlow Quantum Works

The TFQ workflow can be summarized in the following steps:

1. **Quantum Circuit Construction**:
   Use Cirq to define quantum circuits representing the quantum components of your model. These circuits are expressed in a form compatible with TensorFlow.
2. **Encoding Classical Data into Quantum States**:
   Classical data must be encoded into quantum states using quantum feature maps. TFQ provides built-in tools for this purpose, ensuring efficient data preprocessing.
3. **Model Integration**:
   Combine the quantum circuit with classical neural networks or other TensorFlow-based machine learning models. This hybrid design allows quantum circuits to process quantum information, while classical components handle traditional data.
4. **Training and Optimization**:
   Train the hybrid model using TensorFlow's gradient-based optimizers, allowing the quantum parameters to be adjusted alongside classical weights.
5. **Simulation and Deployment**:
   Test the model using Cirq's quantum simulators or deploy it to quantum hardware, such as those offered by Google or IBM, for real-world experimentation.

Benefits of TensorFlow Quantum

- **Seamless Hybrid Modeling**: TFQ simplifies the creation of quantum-classical hybrid models, bridging the gap between quantum computing research and practical machine learning applications.
- **Accelerated Prototyping**: With its integration into TensorFlow, users can rapidly prototype quantum algorithms using familiar tools and workflows.
- **Scalable and Open Source**: As an open-source platform, TFQ is scalable and benefits from a growing community of contributors and users.
- **Accessible Quantum Research**: TFQ democratizes access to quantum computing, enabling machine learning researchers without deep quantum expertise to explore QML solutions.

Beyond TensorFlow Quantum: The Vision

TensorFlow Quantum represents the beginning of a larger shift toward quantum-enhanced artificial intelligence. As quantum hardware continues to evolve, TFQ positions itself as a vital tool for bridging the computational power of quantum systems with the versatility of classical machine learning. It sets the stage for transformative breakthroughs in fields such as cryptography, drug discovery, financial modeling, and artificial intelligence.

In the chapters to come, we'll dive deeper into using TensorFlow Quantum for specific quantum machine learning applications, exploring its unique capabilities to unlock the true potential of quantum intelligence.

Setting Up TensorFlow Quantum

TensorFlow Quantum (TFQ) is a specialized library designed to integrate quantum computing capabilities into the TensorFlow ecosystem. Setting it up correctly is essential for leveraging its full potential in quantum machine learning research and development. This guide provides detailed, step-by-step instructions on installing and configuring TensorFlow Quantum on a local machine or a cloud environment. Additionally, it explains the necessary dependencies, environmental configurations, and troubleshooting techniques to ensure a smooth development experience.

System Requirements and Compatibility

Before setting up TensorFlow Quantum, ensure your system meets the following requirements:

1. **Operating System**: TensorFlow Quantum supports Linux and macOS. Windows users can install it via a compatible Linux subsystem (e.g., WSL 2).
2. **Python Version**: TensorFlow Quantum requires Python 3.8 or higher.
3. **TensorFlow Version**: TensorFlow 2.x must be pre-installed as TFQ extends its functionality.
4. **Cirq Installation**: Cirq, a Python library for quantum circuit simulation, is a prerequisite for TFQ.

For high-performance workloads, a system equipped with GPUs is recommended, especially if running hybrid quantum-classical models that involve intensive classical computations.

Installing TensorFlow Quantum on a Local Machine

1. **Set Up a Virtual Environment**:
   Using a virtual environment is highly recommended to isolate dependencies and avoid conflicts with other Python libraries.

```
bash


python3 -m venv tfq_env
source tfq_env/bin/activate  # On Linux/macOS
tfq_env\Scripts\activate     # On Windows
```

2. **Install TensorFlow**:
   Begin by installing TensorFlow, as it serves as the foundation for TensorFlow Quantum.

```
bash
```

```
pip install tensorflow
```

3. **Install Cirq**:
   Cirq is essential for quantum circuit construction and simulation.

```
bash

pip install cirq
```

4. **Install TensorFlow Quantum**:
   Use pip to install TensorFlow Quantum directly.

```
bash

pip install tensorflow-quantum
```

5. **Verify the Installation**:
   Check if TensorFlow Quantum is installed and working correctly by running the following Python code:

```
Python


import tensorflow as tf

import tensorflow_quantum as tfq


print("TensorFlow version:", tf.__version__)

print("TensorFlow Quantum version:", tfq.__version__)
```

Setting Up TensorFlow Quantum on a Cloud Environment

If local resources are limited, consider setting up TensorFlow Quantum on a cloud platform such as Google Colab, Google Cloud Platform (GCP), or AWS.

1. **Using Google Colab**:
   - Google Colab provides free access to GPUs and is pre-configured for Python-based environments.
   - To install TensorFlow Quantum, execute the following commands in a Colab notebook:

```
Python


!pip install tensorflow

!pip install cirq

!pip install tensorflow-quantum
```

   - Colab also supports Google Cloud integrations, making it easy to access additional resources if needed.
2. **Using Google Cloud Platform (GCP)**:
   - Create a virtual machine with a compatible operating system (Ubuntu is recommended).
   - Install TensorFlow Quantum following the same steps as a local setup.
   - For heavy workloads, configure GPU or TPU instances for accelerated performance.
3. **Using AWS or Azure**:
   - Launch an EC2 instance (AWS) or Virtual Machine (Azure) with a Linux operating system.
   - Install Python and TensorFlow Quantum as described for local machines.
   - Consider leveraging managed ML services like AWS SageMaker for additional scalability.

Configuring the Development Environment

1. **Integrated Development Environment (IDE)**:
   Use an IDE such as PyCharm, VS Code, or Jupyter Notebook for TensorFlow Quantum development. Ensure Python integration and virtual environment support.
2. **Install Additional Dependencies**:
   Depending on the project, you may need additional libraries for data preprocessing, visualization, or hybrid modeling:

```
bash


pip install numpy pandas matplotlib scikit-learn
```

3. **Enable GPU Support** (Optional):
   If your system has NVIDIA GPUs, install the CUDA toolkit and cuDNN libraries to enable GPU acceleration:

```
bash


pip install tensorflow-gpu
```

4. **Set Up TensorBoard for Visualization**:
   TensorBoard is an excellent tool for monitoring and visualizing training metrics in real-time. Install it with:

```
bash


pip install tensorboard
```

Example: Testing TensorFlow Quantum Setup

To validate your TensorFlow Quantum setup, try creating a simple quantum circuit and executing it.

```
Python


import tensorflow_quantum as tfq

import cirq

import tensorflow as tf


# Create a qubit

qubit = cirq.GridQubit(0, 0)


# Create a quantum circuit with a Hadamard gate

circuit = cirq.Circuit(cirq.H(qubit))


# Convert the circuit to a tensor

circuit_tensor = tfq.convert_to_tensor([circuit])


print("Quantum Circuit:")

print(circuit)

print("Circuit Tensor Shape:", circuit_tensor.shape)
```

This script creates a single-qubit circuit, applies a Hadamard gate, and converts the circuit into a tensor representation for integration with TensorFlow models.

Troubleshooting Common Issues

1. **Installation Errors**:
   Ensure pip is updated:

```
bash


pip install --upgrade pip
```

2. **Incompatible TensorFlow Versions**:
   Verify that TensorFlow and TensorFlow Quantum versions are compatible. Check the TFQ GitHub repository for version requirements.
3. **Hardware Limitations**:
   If running on a system without sufficient resources, use cloud platforms with quantum simulation capabilities.

Beyond Installation: Next Steps

Once TensorFlow Quantum is set up, you are ready to:

- Build hybrid quantum-classical machine learning models.
- Simulate quantum circuits for research.
- Integrate quantum operations into advanced AI workflows.

TensorFlow Quantum's robust design and ease of integration make it an essential tool for exploring the frontiers of quantum machine learning. In the next sections, we'll delve into writing practical TensorFlow Quantum models and deploying them on quantum hardware for real-world applications.

Building Quantum Circuits with TensorFlow Quantum (TFQ)

Quantum circuits are the foundational building blocks of quantum algorithms. TensorFlow Quantum (TFQ), in collaboration with Cirq, provides a powerful framework to create, simulate, and integrate quantum circuits into machine learning workflows. This chapter dives into constructing quantum circuits with TFQ, simulating quantum gates and operations, and seamlessly embedding these circuits into TensorFlow models for hybrid quantum-classical processing.

Understanding Quantum Circuits

A quantum circuit is a sequence of quantum gates applied to qubits, the quantum analogs of classical bits. These gates manipulate the quantum states of qubits to perform computations, leverage superposition, and exhibit quantum interference. TFQ uses **Cirq** to define and manipulate quantum circuits, enabling their integration into TensorFlow's ecosystem.

Getting Started with Cirq

Cirq is a Python library designed to create and simulate quantum circuits. It offers tools to define quantum gates, arrange them into circuits, and simulate their behavior on classical hardware. TensorFlow Quantum extends Cirq's functionality, embedding quantum circuits into TensorFlow workflows.

1. **Creating Qubits**:
   Qubits in Cirq are defined on a 2D grid. For example:

```
Python

import cirq

# Define qubits on a 2D grid
qubit_1 = cirq.GridQubit(0, 0)
qubit_2 = cirq.GridQubit(0, 1)

print(qubit_1, qubit_2)
```

2. **Defining Quantum Gates**:
   Common quantum gates include the Hadamard gate (`H`), Pauli gates (`X`, `Y`, `Z`), and controlled gates (e.g., `CNOT`).

```
Python


# Create a single Hadamard gate
hadamard_gate = cirq.H(qubit_1)


# Create a CNOT gate
cnot_gate = cirq.CNOT(qubit_1, qubit_2)
```

3. **Building a Quantum Circuit**:
   A quantum circuit is a sequence of gates applied to qubits.

```
Python


# Build a circuit
circuit = cirq.Circuit()
circuit.append(hadamard_gate)
circuit.append(cnot_gate)


print("Quantum Circuit:")
print(circuit)
```

Integrating Cirq Circuits into TensorFlow Quantum

TFQ allows quantum circuits, defined using Cirq, to be integrated as tensors within TensorFlow models. This enables their use in hybrid quantum-classical workflows.

1. **Converting Circuits to TensorFlow Tensors**:
   Quantum circuits in Cirq are converted into tensors that TFQ can process.

```
Python

import tensorflow_quantum as tfq

# Convert a circuit into a tensor
circuit_tensor = tfq.convert_to_tensor([circuit])

print("Circuit Tensor Shape:", circuit_tensor.shape)
```

2. **Simulating Quantum Circuits**:
   TFQ uses simulators to calculate the output of quantum circuits, either deterministically or probabilistically.

```
Python

simulator = cirq.Simulator()
result = simulator.simulate(circuit)

print("Quantum State Vector:")
print(result.final_state_vector)
```

Building a Quantum Workflow with TFQ

1. **Encoding Classical Data into Quantum States**:
   Quantum circuits often operate on classical data, requiring an encoding step. One popular method is **amplitude encoding**, which maps classical data to the amplitudes of a quantum state.

```
Python


import numpy as np


# Example classical data

data = np.array([1, 0, 1, 0]) / np.sqrt(2)


# Encode the data into a quantum state

encoding_circuit = cirq.Circuit()

for i, bit in enumerate(data):

    if bit == 1:

        encoding_circuit.append(cirq.X(cirq.GridQubit(0, i)))


print("Data Encoding Circuit:")

print(encoding_circuit)
```

2. **Adding Parametrized Gates for Machine Learning**:
   Parametrized quantum gates allow circuits to learn patterns from data, much like weights in a neural network.

```
Python
```

```
import sympy

# Define a parameterized gate
theta = sympy.Symbol("theta")
param_gate = cirq.Ry(theta)(qubit_1)

# Add to the circuit
circuit.append(param_gate)
print("Circuit with Parameterized Gate:")
print(circuit)
```

3. **Constructing a Hybrid Model**:
   Once circuits are defined, they can be embedded into TensorFlow models.

```
Python

import tensorflow as tf

# Define a simple hybrid quantum-classical model
quantum_layer = tfq.layers.PQC(circuit,
tfq.util.random_pauli_sums(1, 1))
classical_layer = tf.keras.layers.Dense(1, activation='sigmoid')

model = tf.keras.Sequential([
    quantum_layer,
    classical_layer
```

```
])


print("Hybrid Model Summary:")

model.summary()
```

Simulating Quantum Gates and Operations

TFQ supports simulation of quantum operations within TensorFlow workflows. For example, a simple Bell state preparation involves applying an H gate and a CNOT gate:

```
Python


# Create a Bell state circuit

bell_circuit = cirq.Circuit(

    cirq.H(qubit_1),

    cirq.CNOT(qubit_1, qubit_2)

)


# Simulate the circuit

result = simulator.simulate(bell_circuit)

print("Bell State Quantum State Vector:")

print(result.final_state_vector)
```

This capability enables researchers to simulate complex quantum behaviors using classical resources.

Practical Applications of TFQ Quantum Circuits

1. **Quantum Kernel Learning**:
   Use quantum circuits to compute kernel functions for machine learning models, such as SVMs.
2. **Hybrid Neural Networks**:
   Combine classical neural networks with quantum circuits to build hybrid models for pattern recognition and anomaly detection.
3. **Quantum Optimization**:
   Simulate variational quantum algorithms like the Variational Quantum Eigensolver (VQE) for solving optimization problems.

Troubleshooting Quantum Circuit Issues

1. **Unphysical States**:
   Ensure all gates are unitary and circuits are properly normalized to avoid invalid quantum states.
2. **Scalability Limitations**:
   Simulating large circuits on classical hardware can be computationally expensive. Consider using cloud-based quantum processors when available.
3. **Debugging Circuit Design**:
   Visualize circuits using Cirq's `plot_circuit_layout()` or similar tools to verify correctness.

Next Steps

With quantum circuit design and simulation integrated into TensorFlow workflows, the next chapter will explore applying these circuits to real-world machine learning problems. You will learn how to fine-tune quantum circuits for specific tasks, deploy hybrid models, and interpret quantum machine learning results.

TensorFlow Quantum bridges the gap between theoretical quantum computing and practical machine learning, empowering researchers and developers to push the boundaries of what is computationally possible.

Hybrid Quantum-Classical Neural Networks with TensorFlow Quantum (TFQ)

Hybrid quantum-classical neural networks represent a transformative paradigm in machine learning, combining the strengths of quantum computing's ability to exploit quantum phenomena, such as superposition and entanglement, with the computational scalability of classical machine learning algorithms. TensorFlow Quantum (TFQ) serves as a bridge between these two worlds, providing tools to design, implement, and evaluate hybrid models seamlessly. This chapter explores the design principles, implementation details, and practical applications of hybrid quantum-classical models using TFQ.

Understanding Hybrid Quantum-Classical Models

In hybrid quantum-classical neural networks, quantum circuits are integrated as layers within classical neural networks. The quantum components perform specialized computations, such as encoding and processing high-dimensional data in quantum Hilbert space, while the classical components handle tasks like gradient-based optimization and large-scale computation.

This integration enables:

1. **Enhanced Feature Processing**: Quantum circuits can encode and process features in ways not possible classically, potentially uncovering patterns hidden in high-dimensional data.
2. **Noise-Tolerant Optimization**: Quantum systems are inherently probabilistic, which may improve generalization and robustness in noisy datasets.
3. **Reduced Computational Complexity**: For specific tasks, quantum components can provide exponential speedups compared to classical algorithms.

Key Components of Hybrid Models in TFQ

1. **Quantum Circuit Layer**: Acts as a feature transformation layer, using quantum gates to process input data encoded in quantum states.

2. **Classical Neural Network Layers**: Perform further feature extraction, decision-making, or regression using traditional neural network architectures.
3. **Parameterization**: Hybrid models include both quantum circuit parameters (e.g., angles of rotation gates) and classical neural network parameters (e.g., weights and biases).

Designing a Hybrid Quantum-Classical Neural Network

The following steps outline the process of building a hybrid quantum-classical model using TensorFlow Quantum:

Step 1: Define the Quantum Circuit

The quantum circuit serves as the quantum layer in the hybrid model. You can define this circuit using Cirq and parameterize it for training.

```
Python


import cirq

import sympy

import tensorflow_quantum as tfq


# Define qubits

qubits = [cirq.GridQubit(0, i) for i in range(2)]


# Define a parameterized circuit

theta = sympy.Symbol('theta')

phi = sympy.Symbol('phi')
```

```
circuit = cirq.Circuit()
circuit.append(cirq.H(qubits[0]))  # Apply Hadamard gate
circuit.append(cirq.CNOT(qubits[0], qubits[1]))  # Apply CNOT gate
circuit.append(cirq.Ry(theta)(qubits[0]))  # Parameterized Ry gate
circuit.append(cirq.Rz(phi)(qubits[1]))  # Parameterized Rz gate

print("Quantum Circuit:")
print(circuit)
```

Step 2: Encode Data into Quantum States

Quantum machine learning requires classical data to be encoded into quantum states. TensorFlow Quantum supports amplitude encoding, angle encoding, and other techniques.

```
Python

import numpy as np

# Classical data to encode
data = np.array([[1.0, -1.0], [0.5, 0.5]])

# Encode data using rotation gates
encoded_circuits = []
for sample in data:
    encoding_circuit = cirq.Circuit()
    encoding_circuit.append(cirq.Ry(sample[0])(qubits[0]))
```

```
    encoding_circuit.append(cirq.Ry(sample[1])(qubits[1]))

    encoded_circuits.append(encoding_circuit)


# Convert to TensorFlow Quantum tensors

encoded_circuit_tensor = tfq.convert_to_tensor(encoded_circuits)
```

Step 3: Define the Hybrid Model

Integrate the quantum circuit as a layer in a TensorFlow neural network. TFQ provides a `PQC` (Parameterized Quantum Circuit) layer for this purpose.

```
Python


import tensorflow as tf


# Define a hybrid quantum-classical model

quantum_layer = tfq.layers.PQC(circuit, cirq.Z(qubits[0]) +
cirq.Z(qubits[1]))  # Expectation layer


model = tf.keras.Sequential([

    quantum_layer,  # Quantum feature extraction

    tf.keras.layers.Dense(16, activation='relu'),  # Classical dense
layer

    tf.keras.layers.Dense(1, activation='sigmoid')  # Output layer for
binary classification

])
```

```
# Print the model summary

print("Hybrid Model Summary:")

model.summary()
```

Step 4: Train the Hybrid Model

Quantum circuit parameters are optimized during training using backpropagation. TensorFlow Quantum handles automatic differentiation for quantum circuits.

```
Python


# Prepare labels for supervised learning

labels = np.array([0, 1])


# Compile the model

model.compile(optimizer='adam', loss='binary_crossentropy',
metrics=['accuracy'])


# Train the model

history = model.fit(encoded_circuit_tensor, labels, epochs=10,
batch_size=2)


# Evaluate the model

loss, accuracy = model.evaluate(encoded_circuit_tensor, labels)

print(f"Model Loss: {loss}, Accuracy: {accuracy}")
```

Applications of Hybrid Quantum-Classical Neural Networks

1. **Quantum-Assisted Feature Extraction**: Enhance feature representation in data-intensive tasks like image classification and natural language processing.
2. **Anomaly Detection**: Detect outliers or anomalies in datasets, especially in financial or cybersecurity domains.
3. **Quantum Kernel Learning**: Leverage quantum circuits for kernel computations in support vector machines (SVMs).
4. **Quantum Optimization**: Solve complex optimization problems in logistics, portfolio management, or chemical simulations.
5. **Quantum Reinforcement Learning**: Use hybrid models for sequential decision-making in environments where quantum systems can accelerate policy evaluation.

Challenges and Practical Considerations

1. **Quantum Hardware Limitations**: Current quantum processors are noisy and limited in the number of qubits, restricting the scalability of hybrid models.
2. **Simulation Overhead**: Simulating quantum circuits on classical hardware is computationally expensive for large circuits or datasets.
3. **Gradient Vanishing**: Similar to classical deep networks, hybrid models can suffer from vanishing gradients, particularly in deep quantum circuits.
4. **Integration Complexity**: Designing efficient data encoding schemes and optimizing hybrid architectures require expertise in both quantum and classical machine learning.

Next Steps

Building a hybrid quantum-classical neural network is a significant milestone in quantum machine learning. To further your understanding, consider:

- **Advanced Architectures**: Explore deeper quantum circuits or more complex hybrid architectures.

- **Real Quantum Hardware**: Experiment with deploying models on real quantum processors using platforms like Google Quantum AI or IBM Quantum.
- **Optimization Techniques**: Study advanced optimization methods for hybrid models, such as quantum-aware gradient descent or variational quantum eigensolvers.

By leveraging TensorFlow Quantum, researchers and developers can design practical, scalable hybrid models that harness the power of quantum computing for transformative applications in machine learning. This integration marks a pivotal step towards realizing the potential of quantum-enhanced intelligence in real-world scenarios.

Practical Use Case: Solving a Classification Problem with TensorFlow Quantum (TFQ)

TensorFlow Quantum (TFQ) opens up opportunities for tackling complex machine learning problems by incorporating the power of quantum computing into traditional workflows. In this section, we will explore how to apply TFQ to solve a real-world binary classification problem, showcasing the design, training, and evaluation of a hybrid quantum-classical machine learning model. The example will demonstrate the use of quantum circuits for feature representation and classical neural networks for classification.

Problem Overview

We aim to solve a **binary classification task** where the goal is to distinguish between two classes of data. For this practical use case, we will use synthetic data that can be encoded into quantum states, enabling us to evaluate the potential advantages of quantum feature maps.

Example Problem: Classify points in a 2D dataset into two categories based on their position relative to a non-linear decision boundary.

Step 1: Dataset Creation

To demonstrate the capabilities of TensorFlow Quantum, we generate a synthetic dataset with two classes that are not linearly separable, making the problem well-suited for quantum-enhanced feature extraction.

```
Python
```

```
import numpy as np

import matplotlib.pyplot as plt


# Generate synthetic data

np.random.seed(42)

class_0 = np.random.randn(50, 2) * 0.5 + [2, 2]  # Class 0 centered at
(2, 2)

class_1 = np.random.randn(50, 2) * 0.5 + [-2, -2]  # Class 1 centered at
(-2, -2)


# Combine the data

data = np.vstack((class_0, class_1))

labels = np.array([0] * 50 + [1] * 50)  # 0 for class_0, 1 for class_1


# Visualize the dataset

plt.scatter(data[:50, 0], data[:50, 1], label='Class 0', alpha=0.8)

plt.scatter(data[50:, 0], data[50:, 1], label='Class 1', alpha=0.8)

plt.legend()

plt.title("Synthetic Dataset for Binary Classification")

plt.show()
```

Step 2: Data Encoding into Quantum States

Quantum machine learning relies on encoding classical data into quantum states. TensorFlow Quantum supports angle encoding, where features are mapped to quantum gate parameters.

```python
Python


import cirq

import tensorflow_quantum as tfq


# Define two qubits for encoding features

qubits = [cirq.GridQubit(0, i) for i in range(2)]


# Define a function to encode classical data into quantum states

def encode_data(sample):

    circuit = cirq.Circuit()

    circuit.append(cirq.Ry(sample[0])(qubits[0]))  # Encode the first
feature

    circuit.append(cirq.Ry(sample[1])(qubits[1]))  # Encode the second
feature

    return circuit


# Encode the dataset

encoded_circuits = [encode_data(sample) for sample in data]


# Convert circuits to TFQ tensors

encoded_circuit_tensor = tfq.convert_to_tensor(encoded_circuits)
```

Step 3: Build the Hybrid QML Model

The hybrid model integrates quantum circuits with classical neural networks. The quantum circuit acts as a feature extraction layer, and the classical layers handle the classification task.

```
Python

import tensorflow as tf

# Define a simple parameterized quantum circuit
theta = sympy.Symbol('theta')
phi = sympy.Symbol('phi')

quantum_circuit = cirq.Circuit()
quantum_circuit.append(cirq.H(qubits[0]))  # Hadamard gate
quantum_circuit.append(cirq.CNOT(qubits[0], qubits[1]))  # CNOT gate
quantum_circuit.append(cirq.Ry(theta)(qubits[0]))  # Parameterized Ry
gate
quantum_circuit.append(cirq.Rz(phi)(qubits[1]))  # Parameterized Rz gate

# Define the hybrid model
quantum_layer = tfq.layers.PQC(quantum_circuit, cirq.Z(qubits[0]) +
cirq.Z(qubits[1]))
model = tf.keras.Sequential([
    quantum_layer,  # Quantum layer
    tf.keras.layers.Dense(16, activation='relu'),  # Classical dense
layer
    tf.keras.layers.Dense(1, activation='sigmoid')  # Output layer for
```

```
binary classification
])


# Model summary
model.summary()
```

Step 4: Train the Hybrid Model

To train the model, we compile it with a binary cross-entropy loss function and an optimizer. The training process optimizes both the quantum and classical parameters.

```
Python


# Compile the model
model.compile(optimizer='adam', loss='binary_crossentropy',
metrics=['accuracy'])


# Train the model
history = model.fit(encoded_circuit_tensor, labels, epochs=20,
batch_size=8)


# Evaluate the model
loss, accuracy = model.evaluate(encoded_circuit_tensor, labels)
print(f"Loss: {loss}, Accuracy: {accuracy}")
```

Step 5: Evaluate and Analyze the Model

Evaluate the model's performance on the training dataset and visualize the decision boundary.

```python
Python

# Predict class probabilities
predictions = model.predict(encoded_circuit_tensor)

# Visualize decision boundary
x_min, x_max = data[:, 0].min() - 1, data[:, 0].max() + 1
y_min, y_max = data[:, 1].min() - 1, data[:, 1].max() + 1
xx, yy = np.meshgrid(np.arange(x_min, x_max, 0.1), np.arange(y_min,
y_max, 0.1))
grid = np.c_[xx.ravel(), yy.ravel()]

# Encode grid points
grid_encoded = tfq.convert_to_tensor([encode_data(point) for point in
grid])
grid_predictions = model.predict(grid_encoded)
grid_predictions = grid_predictions.reshape(xx.shape)

# Plot decision boundary
plt.contourf(xx, yy, grid_predictions, levels=[0, 0.5, 1],
cmap='coolwarm', alpha=0.5)
plt.scatter(data[:50, 0], data[:50, 1], label='Class 0', alpha=0.8)
plt.scatter(data[50:, 0], data[50:, 1], label='Class 1', alpha=0.8)
plt.legend()
```

```
plt.title("Decision Boundary of Hybrid Quantum-Classical Model")
plt.show()
```

Advantages of TFQ for Classification Tasks

1. **Quantum Feature Maps**: The quantum circuits capture complex data relationships that may be difficult to model with classical approaches.
2. **Scalability**: For problems requiring exponential computational resources, quantum approaches can offer significant advantages.
3. **Seamless Integration**: TensorFlow Quantum allows easy integration of quantum components with TensorFlow's powerful ecosystem for model training and evaluation.

Challenges and Practical Considerations

1. **Hardware Limitations**: Simulations on classical machines can be slow, and access to real quantum processors is limited.
2. **Overfitting Risks**: Small datasets can lead to overfitting due to the flexibility of quantum circuits.
3. **Optimization Complexity**: Training quantum parameters requires careful optimization to avoid issues like vanishing gradients.

Conclusion and Future Directions

By solving a binary classification problem with TensorFlow Quantum, this use case demonstrates the practical applicability of hybrid quantum-classical models. As quantum hardware improves, hybrid models could be deployed to tackle larger datasets and more complex problems. Future work might include exploring real-world datasets, designing more sophisticated quantum feature maps, and leveraging quantum processors to test the scalability of these models in production environments.

CHAPTER 5: Qiskit for Quantum Machine Learning

DESCRIPTION:

This chapter explores **Qiskit**, IBM's open-source framework for quantum computing, and its application in quantum machine learning. Readers will learn how to construct quantum circuits, integrate machine learning workflows, and leverage Qiskit's tools to build and train quantum models. Through hands-on examples, the chapter covers the implementation of hybrid algorithms and quantum-classical approaches for real-world machine learning tasks.

Introduction to Qiskit and Its Ecosystem

Qiskit, developed by IBM, is one of the leading open-source quantum computing frameworks, designed to provide a comprehensive environment for building and executing quantum algorithms. Its versatility and modular architecture have made it a popular tool for both researchers and practitioners in the quantum computing field. Qiskit is not just a single library; it's a complete ecosystem composed of several modules, each specializing in different aspects of quantum computing and quantum machine learning (QML).

Qiskit Overview

At its core, Qiskit allows users to design, simulate, and execute quantum circuits on both simulators and real quantum hardware. The framework provides a set of tools that span the entire quantum computing workflow—from designing quantum circuits to running them on actual quantum processors, all while integrating seamlessly with classical machine learning pipelines. It provides an abstraction layer that allows users to work with quantum circuits at a high level, without needing deep hardware-specific knowledge.

The Modular Components of Qiskit

Qiskit's modular structure is one of its standout features. The framework is divided into several key components that each handle different aspects of quantum computing. These modules allow users to easily customize their workflow based on specific needs, whether they are simulating quantum circuits or integrating quantum algorithms into machine learning pipelines.

1. **Qiskit Terra**
   Terra is the foundational layer of Qiskit, responsible for circuit creation, manipulation, and optimization. It provides the basic tools needed for quantum circuit design and allows users to compile, optimize, and execute quantum programs on both simulators and actual quantum processors. It ensures compatibility between various quantum hardware and provides the necessary infrastructure for quantum software development.
2. **Qiskit Aer**
   Aer is the simulator module of Qiskit, providing high-performance simulators for running quantum algorithms. Aer supports a range of simulators, from statevector simulators (which simulate the full quantum state) to noise models and quantum error correction. It enables developers to test their quantum circuits on classical

machines before running them on actual quantum hardware, allowing for debugging and optimization.

3. **Qiskit Ignis**
   Ignis focuses on quantum error correction and noise reduction, crucial for current quantum computers, which are still noisy and prone to errors. This module provides tools for developing techniques to mitigate noise, correct errors in quantum circuits, and enhance the reliability of quantum computations. It includes methods for quantum error correction codes, quantum state tomography, and benchmarking quantum devices.
4. **Qiskit Aqua**
   Aqua is the high-level library in Qiskit aimed at solving real-world problems using quantum algorithms. It contains a set of ready-to-use algorithms that are particularly useful in the realm of quantum machine learning, optimization, chemistry, and artificial intelligence. Aqua allows users to leverage quantum computing for solving industry-specific problems by providing pre-built quantum algorithms such as the Variational Quantum Eigensolver (VQE), Quantum Approximate Optimization Algorithm (QAOA), and more. This makes it particularly useful for those seeking to implement hybrid quantum-classical machine learning models, where quantum algorithms work alongside classical algorithms to solve complex tasks.

Qiskit in Quantum Machine Learning (QML)

The modular components of Qiskit are seamlessly integrated into the domain of quantum machine learning, enabling users to build hybrid quantum-classical models. The core value of Qiskit lies in its ability to combine quantum algorithms with classical machine learning workflows, leveraging quantum properties such as superposition and entanglement to enhance the learning process. Quantum algorithms like the Quantum Support Vector Machine (QSVM), Quantum K-Means, and Variational Quantum Classifiers (VQC) are built using the tools provided by Qiskit, offering new ways to tackle machine learning problems that may be intractable for classical computers.

In particular, Qiskit's **Aqua** module provides pre-built algorithms and tools that can be used for quantum-enhanced machine learning, such as applying quantum circuits for dimensionality reduction or quantum-enhanced optimization, which can outperform classical methods in specific cases.

How Qiskit Fits into the Quantum Ecosystem

Qiskit stands as an essential tool for researchers and practitioners navigating the complex landscape of quantum computing. Its integration with classical machine learning frameworks and ability to execute on real quantum hardware positions it as a critical player in bridging the gap between classical and quantum computing. The ability to design, simulate, and execute quantum circuits on real devices while also optimizing and debugging within a classical environment gives users a powerful toolkit for exploring quantum-enhanced algorithms.

Moreover, Qiskit's modular approach means that it can easily scale with the rapidly advancing field of quantum computing, allowing researchers to build on existing components as the ecosystem expands and new quantum hardware becomes available. As quantum hardware improves and becomes more accessible, Qiskit will continue to serve as a bridge for realizing the full potential of quantum machine learning.

Qiskit's ecosystem, with its robust modules Terra, Aer, Ignis, and Aqua, offers a versatile and comprehensive solution for quantum computing and quantum machine learning. Its integration of quantum algorithms with classical machine learning workflows makes it an ideal framework for developing cutting-edge quantum-enhanced machine learning models. Whether you're developing quantum circuits, simulating quantum algorithms, or applying quantum machine learning to solve real-world problems, Qiskit provides the tools and flexibility needed to explore the exciting potential of quantum computing.

Setting Up Qiskit for Development

To harness the full potential of quantum computing using Qiskit, you need to set up a development environment that supports local experimentation, cloud-based execution, and hands-on interaction with quantum processors. This guide provides detailed steps for installing and configuring Qiskit on your local machine, integrating it with Jupyter Notebooks for an interactive coding experience, and connecting it to the IBM Quantum Experience platform for running quantum circuits on real quantum hardware.

Step 1: Install Python and Essential Tools

Qiskit is a Python-based framework, so having Python installed is the foundation of your development setup.

1. **Install Python**

  - Download the latest version of Python (preferably Python 3.8 or higher) from python.org.
  - Follow the installation instructions for your operating system (Windows, macOS, or Linux). Ensure that the `pip` package manager is included in the installation.

2. **Verify Installation**
   Open a terminal or command prompt and run:

```
bash


python --version

pip --version
```

   These commands should display the installed versions of Python and pip.

Step 2: Install Qiskit

Qiskit is distributed as a Python package and can be installed using pip.

1. **Install the Core Qiskit Package**
   Run the following command in your terminal:

```
bash


pip install qiskit
```

2. **Verify the Installation**
   After installation, verify that Qiskit is working correctly by running:

```
Python


python -c "import qiskit; print(qiskit.__qiskit_version__)"
```

This command should return the version numbers of Qiskit's modules, such as Terra, Aer, Ignis, and Aqua.

3. **Install Additional Dependencies (Optional)**
   If you plan to use specific features such as Qiskit Aer simulators with GPU acceleration, install additional dependencies:

```
bash

pip install qiskit[visualization] qiskit-aer-gpu
```

Step 3: Set Up Jupyter Notebooks for Interactive Development

Jupyter Notebooks provide an excellent environment for writing and visualizing quantum circuits interactively.

1. **Install Jupyter Notebook**
   Use pip to install Jupyter:

```
bash

pip install notebook
```

2. **Launch Jupyter Notebook**
   Start Jupyter Notebook from the terminal:

```
bash

jupyter notebook
```

A browser window will open, displaying the Jupyter Notebook interface.

3. **Test Qiskit in Jupyter**
   Create a new Python notebook in the Jupyter interface. Run the following code to verify the Qiskit installation:

```
Python

from qiskit import QuantumCircuit
qc = QuantumCircuit(2)
qc.h(0)
qc.cx(0, 1)
qc.draw('mpl')
```

4. **Enable Visualizations**
   Qiskit supports visualizing quantum circuits. To ensure this functionality, install the necessary dependencies:

```
bash

pip install matplotlib
```

Step 4: Connect to IBM Quantum Experience

IBM Quantum Experience allows you to run quantum circuits on real quantum hardware. By linking your Qiskit setup to IBM's cloud-based quantum computers, you can move beyond simulators to actual quantum processors.

1. **Create an IBM Quantum Account**
   - Sign up or log in at IBM Quantum Experience.
   - Navigate to the **API Token** section in your account settings and copy your API key.
2. **Install IBM Quantum Provider**
   Install the `qiskit-ibmq-provider` package:

```bash
pip install qiskit-ibmq-provider
```

3. **Authenticate with IBM Quantum**
   Run the following commands in your Python environment to save your API key:

```python
from qiskit import IBMQ
IBMQ.save_account('YOUR_API_TOKEN', overwrite=True)
```

   Replace `'YOUR_API_TOKEN'` with the API key you copied from IBM Quantum Experience.

4. **Test the Connection**
   Verify the connection to IBM Quantum Experience by loading your account:

```python
IBMQ.load_account()
provider = IBMQ.get_provider(hub='ibm-q')
print(provider.backends())
```

   This should return a list of available quantum backends, including simulators and real quantum processors.

Step 5: Configure a Cloud Environment (Optional)

If you prefer a cloud-based development setup, platforms like Google Colab or JupyterHub can host your Qiskit projects.

1. **Use Google Colab**
   - Open Google Colab.
   - Install Qiskit within a Colab notebook by running:

```
Python

!pip install qiskit
```

   - Authenticate with IBM Quantum Experience by using your API key as described above.
2. **Use JupyterHub**
   - Set up a JupyterHub instance on cloud providers like AWS, Azure, or Google Cloud.
   - Install Qiskit on the server and configure IBM Quantum Experience access for all users.

Step 6: Develop and Test Quantum Circuits

With your environment ready, you can begin building and testing quantum circuits. Start with small experiments to familiarize yourself with Qiskit's workflow.

1. **Create and Simulate a Quantum Circuit**

```
Python

from qiskit import QuantumCircuit, Aer, execute
qc = QuantumCircuit(2)
qc.h(0)
qc.cx(0, 1)
simulator = Aer.get_backend('statevector_simulator')
result = execute(qc, simulator).result()
```

```
print(result.get_statevector())
```

2. **Run on Real Hardware**
   Once your circuit is tested, run it on a real quantum backend:

```
Python


backend = provider.get_backend('ibmq_quito')  # Replace with the desired backend

job = execute(qc, backend)

print(job.result().get_counts())
```

Troubleshooting Tips

1. **Dependency Issues**
   If you encounter installation errors, ensure you're using the latest version of pip:

```
bash


pip install --upgrade pip
```

2. **Visualization Errors**
   If circuit visualizations don't render, check that Matplotlib and LaTeX are correctly installed.
3. **Cloud Connection Issues**
   If you're unable to connect to IBM Quantum Experience, verify your API key and internet connection.

Setting up Qiskit for development equips you with a powerful environment to explore quantum computing and machine learning. Whether running simulations locally or experimenting with real quantum hardware via IBM Quantum Experience, your configured setup will enable hands-on development of cutting-edge quantum algorithms. By integrating Qiskit with tools like Jupyter Notebooks and leveraging cloud platforms, you can ensure a seamless workflow that bridges theoretical quantum computing with practical, real-world applications.

Building Quantum Circuits with Qiskit

Quantum circuits are the foundational structures in quantum computing, representing the sequence of quantum operations applied to qubits. With Qiskit, you can design, simulate, and execute these circuits with precision and flexibility, leveraging its Python-based framework. This chapter explores the construction of quantum circuits, programming quantum gates, creating entanglement, and incorporating quantum operations specifically tailored for Quantum Machine Learning (QML) workflows.

What is a Quantum Circuit?

A quantum circuit is a series of quantum gates and operations applied to qubits to manipulate their states. Unlike classical circuits, which process binary values (0s and 1s), quantum circuits operate on qubits, which can exist in superposition and be entangled. These properties enable quantum circuits to perform computations that are infeasible for classical systems.

---

1. Setting Up a Quantum Circuit in Qiskit

Qiskit's `QuantumCircuit` class is the primary tool for building and managing quantum circuits.

Step 1: Import the Required Libraries
Start by importing the necessary components from Qiskit:

```
Python

from qiskit import QuantumCircuit, Aer, execute

from qiskit.visualization import plot_histogram
```

Step 2: Create a Quantum Circuit
To define a quantum circuit, specify the number of qubits and classical bits. For example:

```
Python


# Create a quantum circuit with 2 qubits and 2 classical bits

qc = QuantumCircuit(2, 2)
```

Step 3: Add Gates and Operations
Apply quantum gates to the qubits:

```
Python


# Apply a Hadamard gate to qubit 0

qc.h(0)


# Apply a CNOT gate with qubit 0 as control and qubit 1 as target

qc.cx(0, 1)
```

Step 4: Measure the Qubits
To extract classical outcomes from the quantum circuit, add measurement operations:

```
Python


qc.measure([0, 1], [0, 1])
```

---

2. Key Quantum Gates and Operations

Qiskit provides a variety of gates to manipulate qubits. Below are the most commonly used gates:

Single-Qubit Gates

1. **Hadamard Gate (H):** Places a qubit in superposition.

```
Python

qc.h(0)
```

2. **Pauli Gates (X, Y, Z):** Perform bit flips and phase shifts.

```
Python

qc.x(0)  # X gate (bit flip)

qc.z(0)  # Z gate (phase flip)
```

3. **Rotation Gates (Rx, Ry, Rz):** Rotate qubit states around specific axes.

```
Python

qc.rx(1.57, 0)  # Rotate around the x-axis by 1.57 radians
```

Multi-Qubit Gates

1. **CNOT Gate (CX):** Creates entanglement between qubits.

```
Python

qc.cx(0, 1)  # Qubit 0 controls Qubit 1
```

2. **Controlled-U Gates:** Apply controlled versions of other gates.

```
Python
```

```
qc.crx(1.57, 0, 1)  # Controlled Rx gate
```

3. **Swap Gate:** Swaps the states of two qubits.

```
Python

qc.swap(0, 1)
```

---

3. Simulating Quantum Circuits

Qiskit's `Aer` module provides simulators to test quantum circuits without requiring real quantum hardware.

Step 1: Use the Statevector Simulator
The statevector simulator returns the quantum state of the system.

```
Python

from qiskit import Aer, execute
simulator = Aer.get_backend('statevector_simulator')

result = execute(qc, simulator).result()
statevector = result.get_statevector()
print(statevector)
```

Step 2: Use the QASM Simulator
The QASM simulator provides measurement outcomes as probabilities.

```
Python

simulator = Aer.get_backend('qasm_simulator')
```

```
result = execute(qc, simulator).result()

counts = result.get_counts()

print(counts)
```

Step 3: Visualize Results
Plot the measurement results using Qiskit's visualization tools:

```
Python


from qiskit.visualization import plot_histogram

plot_histogram(counts)
```

---

4. Entanglement in Quantum Circuits

Entanglement is a uniquely quantum phenomenon where the states of qubits become correlated. It's a critical feature for Quantum Machine Learning.

Creating Entanglement

1. Apply a Hadamard gate to one qubit to create superposition.

```
Python


qc.h(0)
```

2. Use a CNOT gate to entangle the first qubit with the second.

```
Python
```

```
qc.cx(0, 1)
```

Testing Entanglement
Simulate the entangled circuit and analyze the results:

```
Python


result = execute(qc, Aer.get_backend('statevector_simulator')).result()

print(result.get_statevector())
```

---

5. Quantum Operations for QML Workflows

In Quantum Machine Learning, quantum circuits often represent feature maps, optimization layers, or data encoders.

Quantum Feature Maps

Quantum feature maps encode classical data into quantum states, enabling quantum kernels for machine learning tasks.

```
Python


from qiskit.circuit.library import ZZFeatureMap


# Create a feature map with 2 qubits and 3 features

feature_map = ZZFeatureMap(feature_dimension=3, reps=2)
```

Parameterized Quantum Circuits

Parameterized circuits allow optimization of quantum gates during machine learning training.

```python
Python

from qiskit.circuit import Parameter

theta = Parameter('θ')
qc.rx(theta, 0)
```

---

6. Best Practices for Building Quantum Circuits

1. **Modular Design:**
   Break large circuits into smaller sub-circuits to improve readability and debugging.

   ```python
   Python

   sub_circuit = QuantumCircuit(1)
   sub_circuit.h(0)
   qc.append(sub_circuit, [0])
   ```

2. **Use Libraries:**
   Leverage Qiskit's pre-built circuit libraries for complex tasks like feature maps and variational algorithms.
3. **Optimize for Hardware:**
   Adapt circuits to match the topology and gate set of your target quantum hardware to reduce errors.

---

7. Running Quantum Circuits on Real Hardware

Once your circuit is designed and tested, you can run it on IBM Quantum Experience hardware.

Submit a Circuit Job

```
Python


from qiskit import IBMQ
IBMQ.load_account()


provider = IBMQ.get_provider(hub='ibm-q')
backend = provider.get_backend('ibmq_quito')  # Choose a hardware backend
job = execute(qc, backend)
result = job.result()
print(result.get_counts())
```

---

8. Challenges and Opportunities in Quantum Circuit Design

1. **Challenges**
   - **Noise:** Quantum hardware is prone to noise, which can degrade circuit performance.
   - **Depth Limitations:** Real hardware has limits on the depth of circuits it can process.
   - **Scalability:** Increasing qubit numbers leads to exponential complexity.
2. **Opportunities**
   - Quantum circuits open avenues for optimization problems, cryptography, and machine learning.
   - Advances in error correction and hardware will expand the scope of feasible quantum algorithms.

Building quantum circuits with Qiskit is an essential skill for leveraging the power of quantum computing. By mastering the construction of gates, entanglement, and operations, and simulating circuits using Qiskit's tools, you can create sophisticated workflows for quantum applications, including Quantum Machine Learning. These circuits form the building blocks of future breakthroughs in computation, offering a pathway to solve problems beyond the reach of classical systems.

Implementing Quantum Machine Learning Models with Qiskit

Quantum Machine Learning (QML) represents a transformative approach in computational science, combining the principles of quantum computing with classical machine learning to solve complex problems efficiently. With Qiskit, you can design and implement hybrid quantum-classical models that take advantage of both quantum circuits and classical neural networks. This chapter provides a comprehensive guide to building QML models using Qiskit, integrating the `Qiskit Machine Learning` libraries, and evaluating hybrid models in practical scenarios.

---

1. Overview of Hybrid Quantum-Classical Models

Hybrid quantum-classical models blend the strengths of quantum computing (e.g., superposition, entanglement) with the established power of classical machine learning. These models typically involve:

1. **Quantum Layers:** Represented by parameterized quantum circuits that encode data or perform quantum transformations.
2. **Classical Layers:** Standard neural network architectures that process outputs from quantum computations.
3. **Optimization Pipeline:** A joint optimization process that updates both quantum and classical parameters during training.

---

2. Prerequisites and Setup

Before building QML models, ensure the following:

- **Install Required Libraries:**
  Install Qiskit Machine Learning and associated dependencies.

```
bash
```

```
pip install qiskit-machine-learning matplotlib
```

- **Import Libraries:**
  Import key modules for building quantum and classical components.

```
Python

from qiskit import QuantumCircuit
from qiskit_machine_learning.circuit.library import TwoLayerQNN
from qiskit_machine_learning.algorithms.classifiers import
NeuralNetworkClassifier
from qiskit.providers.aer import AerSimulator
from sklearn.datasets import make_classification
from sklearn.model_selection import train_test_split
from sklearn.metrics import accuracy_score
```

---

3. Building Quantum Circuits for Machine Learning

Quantum circuits are integral to QML models. A common approach is to design **parameterized quantum circuits**, where parameters are optimized during training.

Step 1: Define a Parameterized Quantum Circuit

A parameterized quantum circuit introduces variables that adjust quantum gates dynamically during training.

```
Python
```

```
from qiskit.circuit import Parameter

# Define a parameterized quantum circuit with 2 qubits
theta = Parameter('θ')
qc = QuantumCircuit(2)
qc.h(0)  # Apply Hadamard to qubit 0
qc.cx(0, 1)  # Entangle qubits
qc.rx(theta, 0)  # Apply parameterized Rx gate to qubit 0
qc.draw('mpl')  # Visualize the circuit
```

---

4. Integrating Quantum Circuits into QML Models

Qiskit Machine Learning provides tools to embed quantum circuits into machine learning workflows. The **`TwoLayerQNN`** is a common example of a Quantum Neural Network (QNN).

Step 1: Initialize the QNN

The `TwoLayerQNN` encodes data into quantum states and applies parameterized gates for learning.

```
Python

from qiskit_machine_learning.circuit.library import TwoLayerQNN

# Define a 2-qubit feature map and ansatz
qnn = TwoLayerQNN(num_qubits=2, feature_map='ZFeatureMap',
ansatz='EfficientSU2', quantum_instance=AerSimulator())
```

Step 2: Combine QNN with a Classical Classifier

QNN outputs can be integrated with classical classifiers, such as a logistic regression or neural network model.

```
Python


from qiskit_machine_learning.algorithms.classifiers import
NeuralNetworkClassifier


# Create a neural network classifier using the QNN

classifier = NeuralNetworkClassifier(qnn)
```

---

5. Data Preparation for Quantum Models

Unlike classical models, quantum models operate on data embedded into quantum states. This requires preprocessing:

Step 1: Generate Data

For simplicity, use synthetic datasets (e.g., binary classification).

```
Python


X, y = make_classification(n_samples=100, n_features=2, n_classes=2,
random_state=42)

X_train, X_test, y_train, y_test = train_test_split(X, y, test_size=0.2,
random_state=42)
```

Step 2: Feature Encoding

Map classical features to quantum states using a feature map, such as the `ZFeatureMap`.

```
Python

from qiskit.circuit.library import ZFeatureMap

# Define a ZFeatureMap for encoding features into quantum states
feature_map = ZFeatureMap(feature_dimension=2, reps=2)
```

---

6. Training and Optimizing Hybrid Models

Step 1: Define the Optimization Pipeline

Qiskit integrates with optimizers like COBYLA, SPSA, or classical optimizers from `scikit-learn`.

```
Python

from qiskit.algorithms.optimizers import COBYLA

optimizer = COBYLA(maxiter=100)  # Define the optimizer
classifier = NeuralNetworkClassifier(qnn, optimizer=optimizer)
```

Step 2: Train the Model

Train the hybrid model using classical datasets mapped to quantum states.

```
Python

# Fit the model
classifier.fit(X_train, y_train)
```

```
# Make predictions

y_pred = classifier.predict(X_test)

print(f"Accuracy: {accuracy_score(y_test, y_pred):.2f}")
```

---

7. Evaluating Quantum Machine Learning Models

Performance Metrics

Evaluate QML models using standard classification metrics such as accuracy, precision, recall, and F1 score.

```
Python


from sklearn.metrics import classification_report


print(classification_report(y_test, y_pred))
```

Simulating Noise and Hardware Constraints

Use noisy simulators or real quantum hardware to assess the model's robustness.

```
Python


from qiskit.providers.aer.noise import NoiseModel


# Add noise to the simulator

noise_model = NoiseModel()

noisy_simulator = AerSimulator(noise_model=noise_model)
```

---

8. Practical Considerations in QML Model Development

1. **Quantum Resources:**
   Quantum models are constrained by qubit availability and gate fidelity. Optimize circuits for hardware constraints.
2. **Data Size:**
   QML models struggle with large datasets due to encoding overhead. Techniques like sampling or dimensionality reduction may help.
3. **Hybrid Optimization:**
   Joint optimization of quantum and classical parameters is computationally expensive. Use optimizers tailored for hybrid workflows.

---

9. Real-World Applications of QML Models

Hybrid quantum-classical models are applicable across domains:

- **Finance:** Portfolio optimization and fraud detection.
- **Healthcare:** Drug discovery and medical imaging.
- **Supply Chain:** Logistics optimization and demand forecasting.

For instance, solving a binary classification problem in finance might involve predicting market trends using quantum-enhanced kernels.

---

10. Challenges and Future Directions

Current Challenges:

- **Scalability:** Limited qubit count and high noise levels in current hardware.
- **Data Encoding:** Efficiently embedding large datasets remains a bottleneck.
- **Optimization:** Hybrid training requires significant computational resources.

Future Opportunities:

- Development of error-corrected quantum computers will unlock larger-scale applications.

- Advances in quantum compilers and hybrid optimizers will streamline model development.

Implementing Quantum Machine Learning models with Qiskit bridges the gap between quantum computing and real-world machine learning. By leveraging tools like parameterized circuits, feature maps, and hybrid architectures, you can explore the untapped potential of quantum-enhanced learning. As quantum hardware and software ecosystems evolve, QML is poised to redefine the future of computational intelligence.

Practical Use Case: Quantum Support Vector Machines (QSVM)

Support Vector Machines (SVMs) are a foundational machine learning algorithm used for classification and regression tasks, particularly excelling in handling high-dimensional and non-linearly separable data through the use of kernels. Quantum Support Vector Machines (QSVMs) enhance the traditional SVM algorithm by leveraging quantum computing to perform kernel evaluations in a high-dimensional Hilbert space more efficiently. This practical use case demonstrates how to implement a QSVM using Qiskit, train it on a dataset, and analyze its performance compared to classical SVMs.

---

1. Overview of Quantum Support Vector Machines

What is QSVM?

A QSVM is an adaptation of the classical SVM algorithm where the kernel computation is performed on a quantum computer. Quantum kernels exploit the superposition and entanglement properties of quantum states to represent data in higher-dimensional spaces, enabling enhanced classification capabilities.

Advantages of QSVM:

- **Efficient Kernel Calculation:** Quantum computers can calculate inner products of high-dimensional feature vectors (quantum states) more efficiently than classical counterparts.
- **Complex Decision Boundaries:** QSVMs can model more complex decision boundaries by mapping data to a richer quantum feature space.
- **Potential Speed-Up:** For certain datasets, QSVMs promise computational advantages over classical SVMs.

---

2. Prerequisites and Setup

To implement QSVM in Qiskit, ensure the following setup:

Install Required Libraries

```
bash


pip install qiskit qiskit-machine-learning scikit-learn matplotlib
```

Import Necessary Modules

```
Python



from qiskit import Aer

from qiskit.circuit.library import ZZFeatureMap

from qiskit.utils import QuantumInstance

from qiskit_machine_learning.algorithms import QSVM

from sklearn.datasets import make_classification

from sklearn.model_selection import train_test_split

from sklearn.metrics import accuracy_score, classification_report
```

Hardware or Simulator

You can execute the QSVM on either a quantum simulator or real quantum hardware. For this demonstration, we'll use Qiskit's Aer simulator.

---

3. Dataset Preparation

QSVMs work with binary classification datasets. For simplicity, we use a synthetic dataset, but real-world datasets (e.g., cancer detection, fraud detection) can also be employed.

Step 1: Generate or Load the Dataset

```
Python


# Create a synthetic binary classification dataset

X, y = make_classification(n_samples=100, n_features=2, n_classes=2,
n_informative=2, random_state=42)


# Split the data into training and test sets

X_train, X_test, y_train, y_test = train_test_split(X, y, test_size=0.2,
random_state=42)
```

Step 2: Normalize the Data

Quantum algorithms typically require normalized data to map features to the range $[0, 2\pi]$.

```
Python


import numpy as np


X_train = np.pi * (X_train - X_train.min()) / (X_train.max() -
X_train.min())

X_test = np.pi * (X_test - X_test.min()) / (X_test.max() - X_test.min())
```

---

4. Quantum Kernel Design

A key component of QSVM is the quantum kernel, which maps classical data into a quantum feature space. In Qiskit, the **`ZZFeatureMap`** is commonly used.

Step 1: Define the Quantum Feature Map

```
Python
```

```
from qiskit.circuit.library import ZZFeatureMap


# Create a feature map with 2 qubits and 2 repetitions

feature_map = ZZFeatureMap(feature_dimension=2, reps=2)

feature_map.draw('mpl')  # Visualize the quantum feature map
```

The `ZZFeatureMap` encodes input features into quantum states using parameterized rotations and entangling gates, creating a quantum kernel.

---

5. Implementing QSVM with Qiskit

Step 1: Initialize the Quantum Instance

The quantum instance handles the execution of quantum circuits on a simulator or quantum hardware.

```
Python


from qiskit import Aer

from qiskit.utils import QuantumInstance


# Use the Aer simulator for execution

quantum_instance = QuantumInstance(Aer.get_backend('qasm_simulator'),
shots=1024)
```

Step 2: Initialize the QSVM

Qiskit's QSVM implementation uses the quantum kernel to classify data points.

```
Python
```

```
from qiskit_machine_learning.algorithms import QSVM


# Initialize the QSVM with the feature map and quantum instance

qsvm = QSVM(feature_map=feature_map, quantum_instance=quantum_instance)
```

Step 3: Train the QSVM

Fit the QSVM to the training data.

```
Python


qsvm.fit(X_train, y_train)
```

Step 4: Predict with the QSVM

Evaluate the trained QSVM on the test data.

```
Python


y_pred = qsvm.predict(X_test)

print(f"Accuracy: {accuracy_score(y_test, y_pred):.2f}")
```

---

6. Evaluation and Analysis

Performance Metrics

Use standard metrics like accuracy, precision, recall, and F1 score to evaluate the QSVM.

```
Python


from sklearn.metrics import classification_report
```

```
# Generate a classification report
print(classification_report(y_test, y_pred))
```

Comparison with Classical SVM

Compare the QSVM results with a classical SVM to evaluate the quantum advantage.

```
Python

from sklearn.svm import SVC

# Train a classical SVM
svm = SVC(kernel='rbf')
svm.fit(X_train, y_train)

# Evaluate the classical SVM
y_pred_classical = svm.predict(X_test)
print(f"Classical SVM Accuracy: {accuracy_score(y_test,
y_pred_classical):.2f}")
```

---

7. Real-World Applications of QSVM

QSVMs can be applied to various domains where kernel-based methods excel:

- **Healthcare:** Classifying diseases (e.g., cancer detection) based on genomic or imaging data.
- **Finance:** Fraud detection and credit risk assessment using complex financial datasets.
- **Material Science:** Predicting material properties based on quantum simulations.

- **Quantum Chemistry:** Molecule classification tasks leveraging quantum kernels for richer feature representation.

For instance, a QSVM can classify patients as either high-risk or low-risk for a disease based on genomic data, potentially outperforming classical methods due to enhanced feature mapping.

---

8. Challenges and Future Directions

Current Challenges:

1. **Hardware Limitations:** Real quantum hardware has limited qubits and high noise levels, restricting scalability.
2. **Execution Overhead:** Kernel computations on a quantum device require numerous circuit executions, increasing runtime.
3. **Data Dimensionality:** Quantum feature maps may not handle high-dimensional datasets efficiently.

Future Opportunities:

1. **Error Mitigation:** Advances in error-correction techniques will improve the reliability of quantum kernel computations.
2. **Quantum-Optimized Kernels:** Development of new quantum feature maps tailored for specific datasets or domains.
3. **Hardware Improvements:** Scalability will improve with more robust and higher-qubit quantum devices.

Quantum Support Vector Machines (QSVMs) provide a glimpse into the potential of quantum computing in machine learning, leveraging quantum kernels to achieve enhanced classification performance. With Qiskit, implementing a QSVM is accessible to developers, enabling experimentation with hybrid classical-quantum models. While current challenges like hardware limitations persist, ongoing advancements in quantum technology promise a future where QSVMs can outperform classical counterparts in practical, real-world applications.

CHAPTER 6: PennyLane for Quantum Differentiable Programming

DESCRIPTION:

This chapter introduces **PennyLane**, an open-source library for quantum differentiable programming that bridges quantum computing and machine learning. Readers will explore how PennyLane enables seamless integration of quantum circuits with gradient-based optimization techniques, making it a powerful tool for building hybrid quantum-classical models. Through hands-on examples, the chapter covers circuit construction, automatic differentiation, and implementing quantum machine learning workflows.

Introduction to PennyLane and Quantum Differentiable Programming

PennyLane is a cutting-edge software library that bridges the gap between quantum computing and classical machine learning through the innovative concept of **quantum differentiable programming**. At its core, PennyLane allows users to seamlessly integrate quantum circuits into traditional deep learning pipelines by enabling automatic differentiation of quantum operations. This capability unlocks the potential to optimize hybrid quantum-classical systems using familiar tools and techniques from classical machine learning.

What is Quantum Differentiable Programming?

Quantum differentiable programming is a paradigm that combines the principles of quantum computing with the powerful optimization techniques of classical machine learning. It enables users to:

1. **Define quantum circuits as differentiable computational graphs**: This means the outputs of quantum circuits can be mathematically connected to their inputs, allowing gradients to be computed automatically.
2. **Leverage gradient-based optimization techniques**: By computing the gradients of quantum circuits, classical optimizers can be used to adjust parameters in hybrid quantum-classical models.
3. **Integrate quantum circuits with classical neural networks**: This hybrid approach combines the strengths of quantum mechanics—such as superposition, entanglement, and exponential scaling—with the versatility of classical neural networks, paving the way for novel solutions to complex problems.

Why PennyLane?

PennyLane is uniquely positioned to be a leader in quantum differentiable programming due to its:

- **Ease of Integration**: PennyLane is designed to work seamlessly with popular machine learning frameworks such as TensorFlow and PyTorch. This compatibility allows data scientists and machine learning practitioners to integrate quantum computing into their existing workflows without requiring specialized quantum expertise.

- **Device-Agnostic Design**: PennyLane supports multiple quantum hardware backends (IBM Q, Rigetti, Xanadu's own photonic processors, and more) as well as quantum simulators. This flexibility enables experimentation on various platforms while remaining hardware-independent.
- **Extensive Functionality**: PennyLane supports a wide range of quantum machine learning, optimization, and simulation tasks, making it a versatile tool for researchers and developers.
- **Focus on Hybrid Models**: PennyLane emphasizes hybrid quantum-classical models, which leverage the strengths of both paradigms to solve problems that neither can address alone.

Core Features of PennyLane

1. **Differentiable Quantum Circuits**: PennyLane makes quantum circuits fully differentiable, enabling parameter optimization using techniques such as gradient descent. This is achieved through methods like the parameter-shift rule, which allows for efficient gradient calculation in quantum systems.
2. **Integration with Classical Frameworks**: Users can combine quantum circuits with classical layers from TensorFlow, PyTorch, or JAX, creating hybrid models where quantum and classical components are optimized together.
3. **Cross-Platform Support**: PennyLane's device-agnostic API allows users to switch between quantum hardware and simulators with minimal code changes.
4. **Customizable Quantum Nodes**: Quantum nodes in PennyLane represent quantum circuits that can be combined with classical computation in a modular fashion, making it easy to build complex hybrid architectures.
5. **Applications in Variational Algorithms**: PennyLane provides tools for implementing variational quantum algorithms like VQE (Variational Quantum Eigensolver) and QAOA (Quantum Approximate Optimization Algorithm), which are central to quantum machine learning and optimization.

PennyLane in Practice: Compatibility with TensorFlow and PyTorch

PennyLane's compatibility with TensorFlow and PyTorch empowers developers to integrate quantum computing into their machine learning workflows. This is achieved by:

1. **Creating Differentiable Quantum Layers**: Users can define quantum layers that interact seamlessly with classical neural network layers, allowing for end-to-end training of hybrid models.
2. **Gradient-Based Optimization**: By leveraging the automatic differentiation capabilities of TensorFlow and PyTorch, users can optimize quantum parameters using standard machine learning optimizers (e.g., Adam, SGD).
3. **Unified Workflows**: Developers can construct, train, and evaluate hybrid models entirely within the TensorFlow or PyTorch ecosystem, ensuring familiarity and ease of use.

PennyLane's Role in Quantum Differentiable Programming

PennyLane stands out as a key enabler of quantum differentiable programming by providing a unified platform for:

- Developing hybrid quantum-classical algorithms.
- Exploring quantum-enhanced machine learning models.
- Experimenting with variational quantum algorithms for optimization and simulation tasks.
- Accelerating research and development in quantum computing by making quantum machine learning more accessible to a broader audience of machine learning practitioners.

Significance and Future Potential

PennyLane is not just a library; it represents a paradigm shift in how quantum computing and machine learning can work together. By enabling quantum differentiable programming, PennyLane opens up new possibilities in:

- **Quantum-Enhanced AI**: Solving problems in areas like natural language processing, computer vision, and recommendation systems by leveraging quantum mechanics.

- **Optimization**: Addressing complex optimization challenges in industries such as logistics, finance, and energy.
- **Scientific Discovery**: Accelerating breakthroughs in materials science, drug discovery, and chemistry through quantum simulations.

As quantum hardware matures, PennyLane will play an instrumental role in making quantum machine learning practical and impactful across industries. For researchers, developers, and businesses alike, it offers a gateway to the future of computation.

Setting Up PennyLane: A Comprehensive Guide

To start your journey into quantum machine learning and quantum differentiable programming with PennyLane, you need to install the library, configure your development environment, and integrate it with quantum simulators and cloud-based quantum hardware providers. This guide offers detailed, step-by-step instructions for a seamless setup process, ensuring you're equipped to leverage the full potential of PennyLane.

---

1. Installing PennyLane

PennyLane can be installed on various platforms, including macOS, Linux, and Windows. Follow these steps to get started:

Step 1: Ensure a Compatible Environment

Before installing PennyLane, ensure you have Python (version 3.8 or later) installed. You can verify your Python version by running:

```
bash


python --version
```

If Python isn't installed or the version is outdated, download and install the latest version from python.org.

Step 2: Install PennyLane via pip

PennyLane is available as a Python package and can be installed using pip. Open your terminal and run the following command:

```
bash

pip install pennylane
```

This command installs the core PennyLane library, which includes its essential quantum differentiable programming functionalities.

Step 3: Verify Installation

After installation, verify it by running the following Python command:

```
Python

import pennylane as qml
print(qml.__version__)
```

If no errors occur and the version number is displayed, PennyLane is successfully installed.

---

2. Installing Additional PennyLane Plugins

PennyLane supports various quantum hardware and simulator backends through plugins. Depending on your development needs, you may want to install the following:

Commonly Used Plugins

- **PennyLane-Cirq**: For integration with Google's Cirq simulator and quantum devices.

```
bash
```

```
pip install pennylane-cirq
```

- **PennyLane-Qiskit**: For integration with IBM's Qiskit and quantum systems.

```
bash

pip install pennylane-qiskit
```

- **PennyLane-Braket**: For integration with Amazon Braket's quantum hardware and simulators.

```
bash

pip install pennylane-braket
```

- **PennyLane-QuTiP**: For simulating open quantum systems.

```
bash

pip install pennylane-qutip
```

Refer to PennyLane's plugin documentation for a complete list of supported plugins.

---

3. Configuring PennyLane for Development

Step 1: Setting Up a Virtual Environment

It's a good practice to create a virtual environment for your project to isolate dependencies. Use the following commands:

```bash
python -m venv pennylane_env
source pennylane_env/bin/activate   # For Linux/MacOS
pennylane_env\Scripts\activate      # For Windows
```

After activating the virtual environment, reinstall PennyLane and any plugins you need.

Step 2: Setting Up Jupyter Notebooks

To experiment interactively with PennyLane, set up Jupyter Notebooks. Install Jupyter by running:

```bash
pip install jupyter
```

Launch a Jupyter Notebook using:

```bash
jupyter notebook
```

Step 3: Configuring Logging and Debugging

Enable PennyLane's logging functionality to debug and monitor quantum circuits:

```Python
import logging
logging.basicConfig(level=logging.INFO)
```

This configuration will provide detailed output during development and help troubleshoot issues.

---

4. Integrating PennyLane with Quantum Simulators

Local Simulators

PennyLane supports several local simulators for experimentation:

- **Default.qubit**: PennyLane's built-in quantum simulator.

```
Python


dev = qml.device("default.qubit", wires=2)
```

- **Cirq Simulator**: For using Google's Cirq library as the backend.

```
Python


dev = qml.device("cirq.simulator", wires=2)
```

Cloud-Based Simulators

PennyLane also supports cloud-based simulators, including IBM Quantum and Amazon Braket.

1. **IBM Quantum Experience**
   - Create an account on IBM Quantum.
   - Generate an API token from your IBM Quantum dashboard.
   - Install Qiskit and set the token in your environment:

```
bash
```

```
pip install qiskit

from qiskit import IBMQ

IBMQ.save_account('YOUR_API_TOKEN')
```

2. **Amazon Braket**
   - Sign up for AWS and set up the Amazon Braket service.
   - Configure AWS CLI credentials:

```
bash


aws configure
```

   - Use PennyLane-Braket to connect to Braket devices:

```
Python


dev = qml.device("braket.aws.qubit", wires=2,
device_arn="YOUR_DEVICE_ARN")
```

---

5. Setting Up PennyLane for Quantum Hardware

PennyLane supports direct integration with several quantum hardware providers:

1. **IBM Quantum Devices**
   With Qiskit installed and your IBM account connected, you can access quantum devices as follows:

```
Python


dev = qml.device("qiskit.ibmq", wires=2, backend="ibmq_manila")
```

2. **Rigetti's Quantum Computers**
   Install the Forest SDK and use PennyLane's Rigetti plugin:

```
Python

pip install pennylane-forest
dev = qml.device("forest.qvm", wires=2)
```

3. **Amazon Braket Hardware**
   Access devices like Rigetti, IonQ, or OQC through Amazon Braket by specifying the `device_arn` in the PennyLane-Braket plugin.

---

6. Testing Your Setup

To verify that everything is configured correctly, create a simple quantum circuit:

```
Python

import pennylane as qml
from pennylane import numpy as np

# Define the device
dev = qml.device("default.qubit", wires=2)

# Define a quantum node
@qml.qnode(dev)
def quantum_circuit(params):
    qml.RX(params[0], wires=0)
```

```
    qml.RY(params[1], wires=1)

    qml.CNOT(wires=[0, 1])

    return qml.expval(qml.PauliZ(0))


# Test the circuit

params = np.array([0.54, 0.12])

print(quantum_circuit(params))
```

---

7. Next Steps

After setting up PennyLane, you're ready to:

- Build custom quantum circuits and hybrid models.
- Experiment with quantum machine learning using classical frameworks like TensorFlow and PyTorch.
- Explore real-world quantum applications, including optimization, simulation, and machine learning.

PennyLane's flexible, modular design empowers you to prototype and deploy hybrid quantum-classical models, enabling innovative solutions across industries. By following this guide, you've laid the groundwork for leveraging quantum differentiable programming at the frontier of computation.

Building Parameterized Quantum Circuits: The Foundation of Variational Quantum Algorithms

Parameterized quantum circuits, also known as variational circuits, are the cornerstone of hybrid quantum-classical algorithms. These circuits combine quantum mechanics with classical optimization techniques to solve complex computational tasks in areas such as machine learning, optimization, and material science. This guide provides an in-depth exploration of parameterized quantum circuits, how to define quantum gates with trainable parameters, and their role in hybrid optimization workflows.

---

1. What Are Parameterized Quantum Circuits?

Parameterized quantum circuits are quantum circuits where certain quantum gates are defined with variable parameters. These parameters are typically optimized during a training process to minimize or maximize a given objective function, such as a cost or loss function in quantum machine learning or variational quantum eigensolvers (VQE).

In a variational approach:

- **Quantum Circuits** perform quantum transformations and computations based on trainable parameters.
- **Classical Optimizers** adjust these parameters iteratively to achieve the desired outcome.

2. Key Components of Parameterized Quantum Circuits

1. **Trainable Quantum Gates**:
   Quantum gates in these circuits depend on parameters that are tunable during the optimization process. Common parameterized gates include:
   - **Rotation Gates**:
     - $R_x(\theta) = e^{-i\frac{\theta}{2}X}$
     - $R_y(\theta) = e^{-i\frac{\theta}{2}Y}$
     - $R_z(\theta) = e^{-i\frac{\theta}{2}Z}$
       These gates rotate the quantum state around specific axes on the Bloch sphere by a parameter θ.
   - **Parameterized Controlled Gates**:
     Such as controlled rotation gates, where the control qubit determines the application of a parameterized rotation.
2. **Entanglement Operations**:
   Gates like $CNOT$ or CZ introduce entanglement between qubits, allowing for complex multi-qubit interactions.
3. **Cost Functions**:
   Defined as classical functions of quantum measurement results, cost functions provide feedback to the optimizer to guide parameter adjustments.
4. **Classical Optimizers**:
   Classical algorithms like gradient descent or Adam optimize the parameters. Hybrid

frameworks often provide automatic differentiation for computing gradients of quantum circuits.

---

3. Constructing Parameterized Quantum Circuits

Step 1: Define the Quantum Device

Choose a quantum device or simulator to execute your circuit. For example, using PennyLane's `default.qubit` simulator:

```
Python


import pennylane as qml

dev = qml.device("default.qubit", wires=3)
```

Step 2: Create a Quantum Node (QNode)

Define a quantum function that uses trainable parameters:

```
Python


@qml.qnode(dev)

def variational_circuit(params):

    # Apply parameterized gates

    qml.RX(params[0], wires=0)

    qml.RY(params[1], wires=1)

    qml.RZ(params[2], wires=2)


    # Introduce entanglement

    qml.CNOT(wires=[0, 1])
```

```
    qml.CNOT(wires=[1, 2])


    # Measure the expectation value
    return qml.expval(qml.PauliZ(0))
```

Here, `params` is a list of trainable parameters that define the circuit's behavior.

Step 3: Initialize Parameters

Before training, initialize parameters randomly:

```
Python


import numpy as np
params = np.random.random(3)  # Initialize 3 parameters
```

Step 4: Execute the Circuit

Run the circuit to obtain the output:

```
Python


output = variational_circuit(params)
print(f"Circuit Output: {output}")
```

---

4. Training Parameterized Quantum Circuits

To optimize parameters, integrate the circuit into a classical optimization loop.

Step 1: Define a Cost Function

The cost function depends on the circuit output. For instance:

```
Python

def cost_function(params):
    return (1 - variational_circuit(params))**2  # Simple squared error
```

Step 2: Optimize Parameters

Use classical optimizers to minimize the cost function. For example:

```
Python

from scipy.optimize import minimize

# Perform optimization
opt_result = minimize(cost_function, params, method="BFGS")
optimal_params = opt_result.x

print(f"Optimized Parameters: {optimal_params}")
```

---

5. Advanced Concepts in Parameterized Quantum Circuits

1. **Gradient Computation**:
   PennyLane supports automatic differentiation for quantum circuits, enabling gradient-based optimization:

```
Python

cost_grad = qml.grad(cost_function)
```

```
gradients = cost_grad(params)
```

2. **Quantum Natural Gradients**:
   A quantum-aware optimization technique that incorporates the structure of quantum states into the optimization process.
3. **Barren Plateaus**:
   Be aware of barren plateaus, where gradients vanish as circuits grow deeper. This phenomenon can be mitigated by careful initialization and circuit design.
4. **Ansatz Design**:
   - **Hardware-Efficient Ansatz**: Designed to match the connectivity of the quantum hardware.
   - **Problem-Specific Ansatz**: Tailored to the structure of the specific problem being solved.
5. **Hybrid Quantum-Classical Workflows**:
   Combine quantum circuits with classical layers in machine learning models. For instance, in a hybrid neural network:
   - Quantum circuits process quantum data.
   - Classical layers refine the output further.

---

6. Applications of Parameterized Quantum Circuits

1. **Quantum Machine Learning**:
   Parameterized circuits are central to quantum neural networks, quantum support vector machines, and other QML models.
2. **Optimization Problems**:
   Variational circuits are used in solving combinatorial optimization problems through algorithms like QAOA (Quantum Approximate Optimization Algorithm).
3. **Quantum Chemistry**:
   VQE leverages parameterized circuits to find the ground-state energy of molecular systems.
4. **Data Encoding**:
   Parameterized circuits encode classical data into quantum states, enabling quantum data analysis.

7. Real-World Example: Building a Variational Classifier

A simple variational classifier for binary classification might look like this:

Step 1: Encode Classical Data

Use parameterized gates to embed classical data into quantum states:

```
Python

def data_embedding(features):
    qml.RX(features[0], wires=0)
    qml.RY(features[1], wires=1)
```

Step 2: Define the Circuit

Combine data embedding with parameterized layers:

```
Python

@qml.qnode(dev)
def classifier_circuit(features, params):
    data_embedding(features)
    qml.RY(params[0], wires=0)
    qml.RY(params[1], wires=1)
    qml.CNOT(wires=[0, 1])
    return qml.expval(qml.PauliZ(0))
```

Step 3: Train the Classifier

Optimize the circuit parameters to minimize the classification error on a labeled dataset.

Parameterized quantum circuits form the backbone of hybrid quantum-classical computing, enabling groundbreaking applications in optimization, quantum chemistry, and machine learning. By mastering their construction and training, you gain the tools to innovate in a rapidly evolving field.

Quantum Gradients and Automatic Differentiation: Leveraging PennyLane for Hybrid Machine Learning

Gradients are at the heart of optimization in machine learning and quantum machine learning (QML). The ability to compute quantum gradients efficiently is essential for training hybrid quantum-classical models. PennyLane stands out in this regard by providing robust automatic differentiation (AD) capabilities for quantum circuits, enabling seamless integration into classical machine learning workflows.

This section explores the principles of quantum gradients, PennyLane's AD features, and how to incorporate these tools into real-world applications.

---

1. Why Are Quantum Gradients Important?

Quantum gradients are derivatives of a cost or loss function with respect to trainable parameters in a quantum circuit. These gradients are critical for optimizing variational quantum circuits in hybrid quantum-classical workflows.

- **Optimization in Quantum Machine Learning**: Training quantum models, such as quantum neural networks or quantum support vector machines, requires gradient-based optimization.
- **Hybrid Quantum-Classical Algorithms**: Algorithms like the Variational Quantum Eigensolver (VQE) and the Quantum Approximate Optimization Algorithm (QAOA) rely on gradients to find optimal parameter configurations.

Efficiently computing these gradients ensures scalability and accuracy when training quantum-enhanced models.

---

2. Challenges in Quantum Gradient Computation

1. **Noisy Environments**: In practical quantum hardware, noise can obscure the gradients, making optimization challenging.
2. **Barren Plateaus**: Variational quantum circuits can suffer from vanishing gradients as the circuit depth increases, hindering optimization.
3. **Finite Sampling**: Quantum measurements are probabilistic, so gradients are estimated using a finite number of samples, which can introduce statistical errors.

---

3. PennyLane's Automatic Differentiation Framework

PennyLane integrates quantum computing with automatic differentiation techniques to provide a powerful framework for computing quantum gradients. This is achieved through backpropagation or parameter-shift rules, depending on the context.

Key Features

- **Unified Gradient Computation**: PennyLane computes gradients for hybrid quantum-classical models seamlessly.
- **Support for Multiple ML Frameworks**: Integrates with TensorFlow, PyTorch, and JAX for end-to-end optimization.
- **Hardware and Simulator Support**: Works across simulators and real quantum hardware providers like IBM Quantum and Rigetti.

---

4. Methods for Computing Quantum Gradients

A. Parameter-Shift Rule

The parameter-shift rule is a quantum-aware differentiation technique that computes gradients using finite shifts of the circuit's trainable parameters.

For a parameterized quantum gate with angle θ\thetaθ, the gradient is given by:

$$\frac{\partial f(\theta)}{\partial \theta} = f\left(\theta + \frac{\pi}{2}\right) - f\left(\theta - \frac{\pi}{2}\right)$$

This approach is exact for circuits with gates that are linear in their parameters, such as RX, RY, RZ.

B. Backpropagation for Hybrid Models

For hybrid models with both classical and quantum components, PennyLane's backpropagation automatically computes gradients through the entire model by leveraging the differentiability of classical layers and quantum circuits.

---

5. Implementing Quantum Gradients with PennyLane

Step 1: Define a Parameterized Quantum Circuit

Create a quantum circuit with trainable parameters using PennyLane:

```
Python


import pennylane as qml

import numpy as np


# Define a quantum device

dev = qml.device("default.qubit", wires=2)


@qml.qnode(dev)

def circuit(params):

    qml.RX(params[0], wires=0)

    qml.RY(params[1], wires=1)
```

```
    qml.CNOT(wires=[0, 1])

    return qml.expval(qml.PauliZ(0))
```

Step 2: Define a Cost Function

The cost function depends on the circuit output. For example:

```
Python


def cost_function(params):

    return (1 - circuit(params))**2
```

Step 3: Compute Gradients with Automatic Differentiation

Use PennyLane's `qml.grad` to compute gradients automatically:

```
Python


grad_fn = qml.grad(cost_function)

params = np.random.random(2)  # Initialize random parameters

gradients = grad_fn(params)

print(f"Gradients: {gradients}")
```

---

6. Training a Hybrid Model with Quantum Gradients

Step 1: Use a Classical Optimizer

Combine the quantum circuit with a classical optimizer, such as gradient descent:

```
Python


opt = qml.GradientDescentOptimizer(stepsize=0.1)
```

```
for i in range(100):  # Training loop
    params = opt.step(cost_function, params)

print(f"Trained Parameters: {params}")
```

Step 2: Hybrid Workflow Integration

Integrate the quantum circuit with classical machine learning frameworks like TensorFlow or PyTorch for advanced workflows:

```
Python

import torch

# Define a PyTorch-compatible quantum node
qml.enable_torch()
qnode = qml.QNode(circuit, dev, interface="torch")

# Initialize PyTorch parameters
params = torch.tensor([0.1, 0.2], requires_grad=True)

# Define a PyTorch loss function
def loss_fn():
    return (1 - qnode(params))**2

# Use PyTorch optimizers
optimizer = torch.optim.Adam([params], lr=0.1)
```

```
# Training loop
for _ in range(100):
    optimizer.zero_grad()
    loss = loss_fn()
    loss.backward()
    optimizer.step()

print(f"Optimized Parameters: {params.detach().numpy()}")
```

7. Advanced Quantum Gradient Techniques

1. **Quantum Natural Gradients**
   Quantum natural gradients use the quantum geometry of parameterized quantum states to improve optimization efficiency. PennyLane supports this method through its `qml.QNGOptimizer`.

```
Python

opt = qml.QNGOptimizer(stepsize=0.1)
params = opt.step(cost_function, params)
```

2. **Higher-Order Differentiation**
   PennyLane enables second-order derivatives for applications requiring Hessians or curvature-based optimization.
3. **Gradient-Free Optimization**
   For circuits with non-differentiable gates, gradient-free techniques like Bayesian optimization can be used.

8. Practical Applications of Quantum Gradients

Quantum Machine Learning

- **Quantum Neural Networks**: Train hybrid neural networks where quantum layers process data features.
- **Quantum Variational Classifiers**: Optimize circuits for binary or multi-class classification.

Quantum Chemistry

- **Variational Quantum Eigensolver (VQE)**: Optimize parameters to find the ground-state energy of molecules.

Quantum Optimization

- **Quantum Approximate Optimization Algorithm (QAOA)**: Optimize problem-specific parameters for combinatorial optimization tasks.

---

9. Key Challenges and Mitigation Strategies

1. **Barren Plateaus**
    - Use shallow circuits to start.
    - Initialize parameters near zero to avoid vanishing gradients.
2. **Noise in Quantum Hardware**
    - Incorporate error mitigation techniques to improve gradient accuracy.
3. **Scaling to Larger Circuits**
    - Use hybrid models to offload computations to classical resources.

PennyLane's automatic differentiation capabilities are transformative for training hybrid quantum-classical models. By integrating quantum gradients seamlessly into machine learning workflows, PennyLane empowers researchers and developers to unlock the full potential of quantum machine learning. Mastery of these tools will enable you to build and optimize sophisticated quantum-enhanced solutions across diverse fields, from artificial intelligence to quantum chemistry.

Practical Use Case: Quantum Neural Networks (QNNs) with PennyLane

Quantum Neural Networks (QNNs) are hybrid quantum-classical models that leverage the strengths of quantum computing to process data in ways that classical systems cannot. These models integrate variational quantum circuits (VQCs) as layers within traditional machine learning architectures. This section will guide you through designing and implementing a QNN using PennyLane, training the hybrid model on a supervised learning task, and analyzing its performance on real or simulated datasets.

---

1. What Are Quantum Neural Networks (QNNs)?

A Quantum Neural Network (QNN) consists of:

- **Quantum Layers:** Parameterized quantum circuits (PQCs) serve as quantum layers, applying unitary transformations to input data and generating quantum states.
- **Classical Layers:** Classical layers process outputs from the quantum layers, enabling hybrid quantum-classical optimization.

Key Advantages of QNNs:

1. **Quantum Feature Mapping:** QNNs map classical input data into a high-dimensional quantum Hilbert space, potentially offering advantages for data separability in machine learning tasks.
2. **Parameter Reduction:** QNNs use fewer parameters compared to large classical neural networks.
3. **Quantum Entanglement:** Entanglement between qubits allows QNNs to learn complex correlations in data.

---

2. Overview of the Workflow

Step 1: Data Preparation

- Use real or simulated data for a supervised learning task (e.g., classification or regression).
- Preprocess the data for quantum circuits, including feature scaling or encoding into quantum states.

Step 2: Model Architecture

- Construct a variational quantum circuit for the quantum layer.
- Combine quantum layers with classical neural network layers to form a hybrid model.

Step 3: Training and Optimization

- Use PennyLane's automatic differentiation to compute quantum gradients for hybrid optimization.
- Train the QNN using gradient-based optimizers like Adam or SGD.

Step 4: Evaluation

- Analyze the model's performance using metrics such as accuracy, precision, recall, or loss.

---

3. Implementing a QNN with PennyLane

Step 1: Import Required Libraries

```python
Python


import pennylane as qml

from pennylane import numpy as np

from sklearn.datasets import make_moons

from sklearn.model_selection import train_test_split

from sklearn.preprocessing import MinMaxScaler

import torch
```

Step 2: Prepare the Dataset

Use a toy dataset for binary classification, such as the "Moons" dataset from scikit-learn.

```python
Python


# Generate a toy dataset

X, y = make_moons(n_samples=100, noise=0.1, random_state=42)


# Normalize the features to the range [0, π] for quantum encoding

scaler = MinMaxScaler(feature_range=(0, np.pi))

X_scaled = scaler.fit_transform(X)


# Split the dataset

X_train, X_test, y_train, y_test = train_test_split(X_scaled, y,
test_size=0.3, random_state=42)
```

Step 3: Define the Quantum Device

Create a quantum device using PennyLane's `default.qubit` simulator.

```python
Python


dev = qml.device("default.qubit", wires=2)
```

Step 4: Build the Quantum Circuit

Construct a parameterized quantum circuit that acts as the quantum layer of the QNN.

```python
Python

```

```
@qml.qnode(dev, interface="torch")
def quantum_circuit(params, x):
    # Encode classical data into quantum states
    qml.AngleEmbedding(x, wires=range(2), rotation="Y")

    # Variational layers
    qml.RY(params[0], wires=0)
    qml.RY(params[1], wires=1)
    qml.CNOT(wires=[0, 1])

    # Return the expectation value
    return qml.expval(qml.PauliZ(0))
```

Step 5: Define the Hybrid Quantum-Classical Model

Combine the quantum circuit with classical layers using PyTorch.

```
Python

class HybridQNN(torch.nn.Module):
    def __init__(self):
        super().__init__()
        self.quantum_params = torch.nn.Parameter(torch.tensor([0.1, 0.2],
requires_grad=True))
        self.linear = torch.nn.Linear(1, 1)  # Classical linear layer

    def forward(self, x):
```

```
        # Apply the quantum circuit

        q_out = torch.stack([quantum_circuit(self.quantum_params, xi) for
xi in x])

        # Combine with classical processing

        return self.linear(q_out)
```

Step 6: Train the Model

Define the training loop with loss function and optimizer.

```
Python


# Initialize the model

model = HybridQNN()

optimizer = torch.optim.Adam(model.parameters(), lr=0.1)

loss_fn = torch.nn.BCEWithLogitsLoss()


# Convert data to PyTorch tensors

X_train_torch = torch.tensor(X_train, dtype=torch.float32)

y_train_torch = torch.tensor(y_train, dtype=torch.float32)


# Training loop

for epoch in range(100):

    optimizer.zero_grad()

    predictions = model(X_train_torch)

    loss = loss_fn(predictions.squeeze(), y_train_torch)

    loss.backward()
```

```
    optimizer.step()


    if (epoch + 1) % 10 == 0:

        print(f"Epoch {epoch + 1}: Loss = {loss.item()}")
```

Step 7: Evaluate the Model

Test the trained model on unseen data and analyze its performance.

```
Python


# Convert test data to PyTorch tensors

X_test_torch = torch.tensor(X_test, dtype=torch.float32)

y_test_torch = torch.tensor(y_test, dtype=torch.float32)


# Evaluate the model

with torch.no_grad():

    test_predictions = model(X_test_torch)

    test_predictions = torch.sigmoid(test_predictions).squeeze()

    test_predictions = (test_predictions > 0.5).float()


accuracy = (test_predictions == y_test_torch).float().mean()

print(f"Test Accuracy: {accuracy.item() * 100:.2f}%")
```

---

4. Advanced QNN Techniques

A. Quantum Circuit Optimization

1. **Layer Depth:** Experiment with deeper quantum circuits for higher representational power.
2. **Ansatz Design:** Use problem-specific ansätze to improve optimization.

B. Noise Mitigation

Train the QNN on noisy simulators or real quantum hardware with error mitigation techniques, such as zero-noise extrapolation or measurement error correction.

C. Hybrid Architectures

Combine QNNs with deep classical networks (e.g., CNNs or RNNs) for tasks involving complex data like images or time series.

---

5. Real-World Applications of QNNs

1. **Image Classification**
   - QNNs can process feature embeddings extracted by classical convolutional layers for improved classification accuracy.
2. **Quantum Chemistry**
   - Use QNNs to model molecular properties and predict chemical reactions.
3. **Financial Analysis**
   - Apply QNNs to portfolio optimization and risk analysis by learning quantum-enhanced patterns in financial data.
4. **Healthcare**
   - Employ QNNs for drug discovery or medical diagnosis tasks, leveraging quantum systems to analyze vast datasets.

---

6. Challenges and Best Practices

1. **Gradient Vanishing (Barren Plateaus):**
   - Use shallow circuits and careful initialization to avoid barren plateaus.

2. **Limited Qubits:**
   - Optimize hybrid workflows to maximize the use of quantum resources.
3. **Noisy Hardware:**
   - Test models on both noisy simulators and real devices to understand their robustness.

By leveraging PennyLane's seamless hybrid integration, Quantum Neural Networks provide a powerful tool for supervised learning tasks. They enable quantum enhancements for real-world applications while working synergistically with classical systems. Mastering QNNs offers a glimpse into the transformative potential of quantum computing in machine learning and beyond.

CHAPTER 7: Quantum Machine Learning with Amazon Braket

DESCRIPTION:
This chapter explores **Amazon Braket**, a fully managed quantum computing service from AWS that provides access to quantum simulators and hardware. Readers will learn how to use Amazon Braket to build, simulate, and run quantum machine learning (QML) models on real quantum devices. The chapter covers setting up the Braket environment, creating quantum circuits, integrating QML workflows, and deploying hybrid quantum-classical algorithms at scale.

Introduction to Amazon Braket and Its Ecosystem

Amazon Braket is a fully managed quantum computing service provided by Amazon Web Services (AWS) that aims to democratize access to quantum computing for researchers, developers, and businesses. Braket serves as a comprehensive platform that allows users to build, test, and execute quantum algorithms, providing a seamless interface between classical systems and quantum hardware. It simplifies the complex and often costly process of quantum computing by offering access to a diverse range of quantum computing resources, from quantum hardware to simulators and hybrid quantum-classical systems. Through Amazon Braket, users can experiment with and leverage cutting-edge quantum technologies to solve real-world problems.

Key Features and Architecture of Amazon Braket

Amazon Braket offers a robust suite of features that make it an indispensable tool for quantum machine learning and quantum algorithm development. Here is an overview of its essential components:

1. **Quantum Hardware Access:** Amazon Braket provides access to quantum processors from multiple hardware providers, including:
    - **D-Wave** for quantum annealing-based approaches.
    - **IonQ** and **Rigetti** for gate-based quantum computing systems. This diverse hardware support enables users to explore different quantum computing paradigms and algorithms based on their specific requirements, such as optimization problems (D-Wave) or quantum circuit-based tasks (IonQ, Rigetti).
2. **Quantum Simulators:** Amazon Braket offers both local and cloud-based quantum simulators that emulate quantum processors on classical hardware. These simulators allow users to prototype and test quantum algorithms without requiring immediate access to actual quantum hardware. Amazon Braket's simulators are particularly useful for early-stage development and debugging of quantum circuits.
3. **Quantum Machine Learning Integration:** The platform's ecosystem is built to support the integration of quantum computing with machine learning workflows. Braket provides tools and libraries that enable the creation of hybrid quantum-classical models, which are essential for practical applications in quantum machine learning (QML). Users can combine quantum circuit-based processing with classical machine learning models to enhance computational power and solve

problems that are otherwise difficult or impossible to address with classical methods alone.

4. **AWS Ecosystem Integration:** Amazon Braket seamlessly integrates with other AWS services such as **Amazon S3** for data storage, **AWS Lambda** for orchestration, and **AWS SageMaker** for machine learning model development. This integration creates a unified environment where users can build, run, and scale their quantum machine learning applications on the cloud, leveraging AWS's powerful cloud infrastructure.
5. **Quantum Circuit Development and Execution:** Amazon Braket supports multiple programming languages and frameworks, such as Python, enabling quantum circuit construction using familiar programming paradigms. With Braket, users can design quantum circuits, compile them, and run them on the selected quantum hardware or simulator. This flexibility supports a wide range of quantum algorithms, including those used for optimization, machine learning, and cryptography.

Amazon Braket's Role in Quantum Machine Learning

Amazon Braket's primary role in quantum machine learning is to provide the necessary infrastructure and tools for the efficient development and execution of quantum-enhanced machine learning models. The platform enables researchers to build hybrid quantum-classical models where quantum circuits are used to perform computations that classical systems cannot efficiently handle.

1. **Hybrid Quantum-Classical Models:** Quantum machine learning often relies on hybrid models that combine quantum and classical components. Amazon Braket allows users to implement these models by connecting quantum computing resources with classical machine learning algorithms. For example, quantum circuits can be used for feature extraction or dimensionality reduction, and classical machine learning models can be used for training and evaluation. This hybrid approach allows the quantum systems to provide speed-ups in areas such as pattern recognition, optimization, and classification, where classical algorithms may struggle due to computational complexity.
2. **Quantum Optimization and Machine Learning:** Many quantum algorithms designed to solve optimization problems, such as **Quantum Approximate Optimization Algorithm (QAOA)** or **Quantum Support Vector Machines (QSVM)**, have applications in machine learning tasks such as classification,

regression, and clustering. Braket's access to both quantum annealers (like D-Wave) and gate-based quantum processors provides researchers the flexibility to experiment with and implement these algorithms for practical machine learning problems.

Bringing Quantum Computing to the Masses:

Amazon Braket's significance lies in its ability to lower the barrier to entry for quantum computing. Traditionally, working with quantum hardware has been difficult due to its high costs, complex programming languages, and limited availability of hardware. Braket's pay-as-you-go pricing model and cloud-based infrastructure address these challenges, enabling users to run quantum algorithms without significant upfront investment in hardware or specialized infrastructure.

The platform's accessibility, in conjunction with AWS's cloud resources, allows both academic researchers and industry professionals to explore and build quantum applications. Braket supports a wide range of use cases, from academic research in quantum algorithms to practical applications in fields like finance, pharmaceuticals, logistics, and machine learning.

Amazon Braket represents a transformative step in the journey of quantum computing by providing users with seamless access to quantum hardware and simulators, simplifying the quantum programming process, and integrating quantum systems into classical workflows. For quantum machine learning, Braket offers a powerful, flexible, and scalable platform to explore hybrid quantum-classical models, enabling groundbreaking research and development in this exciting field. As quantum hardware and algorithms evolve, Amazon Braket will continue to play a pivotal role in bridging the gap between classical and quantum computing, shaping the future of quantum machine learning and other advanced quantum applications.

Setting Up Amazon Braket on AWS: A Detailed Guide

Setting up Amazon Braket on AWS involves several steps to configure the environment, ensure proper access permissions, set up quantum resources, and integrate cloud-based simulators for quantum algorithm development. In this process, you will establish a secure, scalable, and efficient quantum computing environment that facilitates the creation, testing, and execution of quantum machine learning models and other quantum algorithms. This guide will walk through the core steps involved in configuring Amazon Braket on AWS, ensuring a smooth transition from traditional computing to quantum resources.

---

1. Prerequisites for Setting Up Amazon Braket

Before you begin the setup process, ensure the following prerequisites:

- **AWS Account:** You need an active AWS account. If you do not have one, you can create it by signing up on the AWS website.
- **IAM Role/Permissions:** Set up the appropriate Identity and Access Management (IAM) roles to grant permission for accessing Amazon Braket resources.
- **AWS CLI (Optional):** Install the AWS Command Line Interface (CLI) to manage AWS resources via the terminal (optional but recommended for advanced users).
- **Python & Boto3 Library:** Amazon Braket integrates with Python, so you will need Python installed, along with the Boto3 library (AWS SDK for Python) to interact with AWS resources.

---

2. Configuring IAM Permissions and Roles

The first step in the setup process is configuring **AWS IAM** to grant access to Amazon Braket. Proper permissions are required to interact with Braket's APIs, create quantum resources, and manage the quantum hardware and simulators. Follow these steps to configure IAM:

1. **Create an IAM Policy for Amazon Braket:**
   - Navigate to the IAM console within AWS.
   - Click on **Policies** in the sidebar and then choose **Create Policy**.
   - Use the **JSON** editor to paste the following permissions:

```
JSON

{
  "Version": "2012-10-17",
  "Statement": [
```

```
    {
      "Effect": "Allow",
      "Action": [
        "braket:SearchDevices",
        "braket:CreateQuantumTask",
        "braket:DescribeQuantumTask",
        "braket:GetQuantumTask",
        "braket:CancelQuantumTask",
        "braket:ListQuantumTasks",
        "braket:GetDevice",
        "braket:ListDevices"
      ],
      "Resource": "*"
    }
  ]
}
```

- This policy will enable access to Amazon Braket's essential services like searching for devices, creating quantum tasks, and managing tasks on quantum hardware and simulators.

2. **Create an IAM Role for Braket:**
   - In the IAM console, go to **Roles** and select **Create Role**.
   - Choose **AWS service** as the trusted entity and select **Braket** as the service.
   - Attach the custom IAM policy you created earlier to this role.
   - Provide a name for your role (e.g., `AmazonBraketAccessRole`) and finalize the creation.
3. **Attach the IAM Role to Your User or Application:**

- Assign the role to your user or application that will be interacting with Amazon Braket. Ensure that all users or services that need to interact with Braket have the appropriate permissions.

---

3. Setting Up Resources in Amazon Braket

Once IAM roles and permissions are configured, the next step is to set up Amazon Braket resources for quantum computing. This includes selecting quantum devices and configuring the environment to use cloud-based quantum simulators and hardware.

1. **Create a Braket Quantum Device:**
    - Log into the AWS Management Console and navigate to Amazon Braket.
    - Go to the **Devices** section where you can view available quantum devices. These could be simulators or actual quantum processors from partners such as **IonQ**, **Rigetti**, and **D-Wave**.
    - Choose a quantum device based on your algorithm requirements. For example:
        - **Quantum Simulators** for testing algorithms in a classical environment.
        - **Gate-based Quantum Computers** for experimenting with algorithms like QAOA, VQE, and quantum circuits.
        - **Quantum Annealers** (like D-Wave) for optimization problems.
2. **Launch Cloud-Based Simulators (Optional):**
    - To simulate quantum circuits without a physical quantum device, you can use Amazon Braket's cloud-based simulators.
    - Select **Amazon Braket Simulator** from the **Devices** section, where you can choose between various options (e.g., **local simulator** or **cloud simulator**).
    - Simulators are essential for development and debugging, providing users a cost-effective way to test algorithms.
3. **Configure Resource Allocation:**
    - Set up the resources needed for your quantum tasks, such as the number of qubits, execution time, and the quantum algorithm to be executed. You can specify the exact device or simulator you want to use, along with job parameters.

---

4. Setting Up the Development Environment

To begin developing quantum algorithms, ensure that your development environment is correctly configured. You can work directly from the **AWS Management Console**, but many users prefer to use Python-based interfaces and integrate with local development tools like **Jupyter Notebooks** or **AWS Cloud9** for seamless coding and experimentation.

1. **Install AWS SDK (Boto3) for Python:**
   - To interact with Braket from Python, install the **Boto3** library via pip:

   ```
   bash

   pip install boto3
   ```

   - Use **Boto3** to create, monitor, and manage quantum tasks in Braket.
2. **Install Amazon Braket SDK:**
   - For easier interaction with Amazon Braket, install the **Amazon Braket SDK**:

   ```
   bash

   pip install amazon-braket-sdk
   ```

   - The SDK simplifies the process of creating quantum tasks, accessing quantum devices, and managing execution jobs.
3. **Configure Braket with AWS CLI:**
   - Set up AWS CLI if you plan to manage resources directly through the terminal:

   ```
   bash

   aws configure
   ```

   - Provide your AWS credentials, region, and output format when prompted.
4. **Create and Run a Sample Quantum Task:**

- To verify everything is set up correctly, create a sample quantum task using the SDK. Here's an example of submitting a quantum task to a simulator:

```
Python


from amazon_braket_sdk import Braket
import boto3


client = boto3.client('braket', region_name='us-west-2')
task = client.create_quantum_task(
    device_arn='arn:aws:braket:us-west-2:device',
    action='run_task',
    parameters={'qubits': 5}
)
print(f'Task created: {task}')
```

---

5. Working with Amazon Braket for Quantum Machine Learning

Once the Braket environment is set up, you can begin developing and testing quantum machine learning models. Braket supports hybrid quantum-classical models, which are ideal for quantum-enhanced machine learning tasks.

- **Hybrid Models:** Use Braket's quantum devices for executing quantum sub-circuits and classical resources for machine learning tasks, such as model training, feature selection, and hyperparameter tuning.
- **Integration with ML Libraries:** Amazon Braket can be integrated with existing machine learning frameworks like TensorFlow and PyTorch to create hybrid quantum-classical workflows for QML tasks.

---

6. Monitoring and Debugging Quantum Tasks

Amazon Braket provides detailed logs and results for monitoring the performance of quantum tasks. You can track the execution of quantum algorithms, view job status, and analyze the output. Use the AWS Console or Python scripts to query task results, retrieve quantum circuit outputs, and debug any issues.

Setting up Amazon Braket on AWS provides the necessary tools and infrastructure for quantum algorithm development. By configuring IAM permissions, setting up quantum hardware resources, and integrating quantum simulators, users can create a secure, efficient, and scalable environment for their quantum tasks. Additionally, Amazon Braket's integration with Python-based SDKs and AWS's ecosystem makes it a powerful platform for developing hybrid quantum-classical machine learning models and solving complex computational problems with quantum computing.

Building and Simulating Quantum Circuits with Braket SDK

The Braket SDK, developed by Amazon, offers an intuitive and powerful interface for building and simulating quantum circuits. It serves as a bridge between the classical world of computation and the emerging quantum ecosystem, allowing quantum algorithms to be developed, tested, and executed on a variety of quantum hardware and simulators. This guide outlines how to use the Braket SDK to construct quantum circuits, simulate quantum operations, and execute workflows compatible with quantum simulators and hardware backends. It also explores strategies for ensuring the compatibility and efficiency of quantum circuits in different computational environments.

---

1. Understanding the Braket SDK

The Braket SDK provides the necessary tools for building, simulating, and running quantum circuits. It integrates seamlessly with Amazon Braket's quantum simulators and hardware backends, enabling the execution of quantum tasks and real-time analysis of results. The SDK is designed to handle quantum operations such as gates, entanglement, and superposition, providing an abstraction layer that allows users to work with quantum computing concepts through Python.

Key features of the Braket SDK include:

- **Quantum Circuit Construction:** Tools to define quantum circuits using gates and measurements.
- **Simulation Support:** Quantum circuit simulation using classical resources.
- **Hardware Access:** Interface for executing quantum circuits on real quantum devices via Amazon Braket.
- **Hybrid Quantum-Classical Integration:** Ability to create hybrid models by combining quantum and classical resources, ideal for quantum machine learning (QML).

---

2. Setting Up the Braket SDK for Development

Before beginning to build and simulate quantum circuits, ensure that the Braket SDK and its dependencies are installed and configured:

1. **Install the Braket SDK and Dependencies:** Begin by installing the Braket SDK and Boto3 (AWS's SDK for Python), which will allow you to interact with Amazon Braket's services:

```
bash


pip install amazon-braket-sdk boto3
```

2. **Set Up AWS Credentials:** Configure your AWS CLI to ensure that the SDK can communicate with your AWS account:

```
bash


aws configure
```

   Provide your AWS Access Key, Secret Key, and region when prompted.

3. **Verify Installation:** After installation, ensure the SDK is correctly installed by importing it in a Python script or Jupyter Notebook:

```
Python

import amazon_braket_sdk as braket
```

---

3. Constructing Quantum Circuits with Braket SDK

Building a quantum circuit involves specifying quantum gates, quantum registers, and the flow of quantum operations. The Braket SDK allows users to define quantum operations in a high-level way, abstracting the complexities of low-level quantum programming. Here's how to create and manipulate quantum circuits using Braket:

1. **Create a Quantum Circuit:** The primary object for quantum circuit construction in Braket is the `QuantumCircuit` class. It represents the quantum operations and registers in a circuit. To create a basic quantum circuit with two qubits, you can use the following Python code:

```
Python


from amazon_braket_sdk import QuantumCircuit


# Create a new quantum circuit with two qubits
qc = QuantumCircuit(2)


# Apply quantum gates
qc.h(0)  # Apply Hadamard gate on qubit 0
qc.cx(0, 1)  # Apply CNOT gate with control qubit 0 and target
qubit 1


# Display the quantum circuit
```

```
print(qc)
```

2. **Add Quantum Gates:** Quantum circuits are built using quantum gates, which manipulate qubits. Common gates include:
    - **Hadamard Gate (H):** Creates a superposition state.
    - **Pauli Gates (X, Y, Z):** Perform bit-flips and other rotations.
    - **CNOT Gate (CX):** A two-qubit gate for entanglement.
    - **Rotation Gates (Rx, Ry, Rz):** Rotate qubits around specified axes. The Braket SDK allows you to apply these gates and more:

```
Python


qc.rx(0, 0.5)  # Rotate qubit 0 by 0.5 radians

qc.rz(1, 1.0)  # Rotate qubit 1 by 1.0 radians
```

3. **Quantum Measurement:** Measurement is a crucial operation in quantum computing, as it collapses the quantum state into a definite value (0 or 1). The `measure()` method in Braket allows for measurement operations:

```
Python


qc.measure([0, 1])  # Measure both qubits
```

4. **Circuit Visualization:** After constructing the circuit, you can visualize it to gain insights into the quantum operations:

```
Python

qc.draw()
```

4. Simulating Quantum Circuits with Braket SDK

Once a quantum circuit is defined, it can be simulated using Amazon Braket's built-in simulators. This allows for the testing of quantum circuits on classical hardware before executing on actual quantum devices. Braket provides both local and cloud simulators, depending on the complexity of the circuit and available resources.

1. **Choose a Quantum Simulator:** Braket provides multiple simulation options, such as:
    - **Local Simulator:** Runs on your local machine using the Python SDK for small to medium circuits.
    - **Amazon Braket Simulator:** Cloud-based simulator for larger, more complex circuits.
2. **Simulate the Quantum Circuit:** Use the `device` class in Braket to simulate quantum circuits. Here's an example of running the quantum circuit on the simulator:

```
Python

from amazon_braket_sdk import LocalSimulator

# Set up the simulator
simulator = LocalSimulator()

# Run the circuit on the simulator
result = simulator.run(qc).result()

# Get the measurement results
print("Measurement Results:", result.measurements)
```

3. **Simulating Large Circuits on Cloud-Based Simulators:** For larger circuits, you can offload the simulation to a cloud-based simulator using Amazon Braket. First, ensure that you select the correct simulator based on your needs:

```
Python

from amazon_braket_sdk import BraketSimulator

# Use Braket's cloud simulator
cloud_simulator = BraketSimulator()

# Run the quantum circuit on the cloud simulator
result = cloud_simulator.run(qc).result()
print(result.measurements)
```

4. **Accessing Execution Logs:** While running the quantum circuit on either local or cloud simulators, you can access execution logs to debug and improve your circuit. These logs will help you track issues such as gate errors, state collapses, and execution time.

---

5. Working with Quantum Hardware Backends

After validating and optimizing quantum circuits on simulators, the next step is to execute them on real quantum hardware. Amazon Braket allows you to access quantum devices provided by hardware partners like IonQ, Rigetti, and D-Wave, offering a range of capabilities from gate-based quantum computing to quantum annealing.

1. **Choose a Quantum Hardware Device:** Depending on your algorithm and the specific task at hand, choose a hardware device from one of Braket's supported partners. You can view available devices through the AWS Console or using the Braket SDK:

```python
Python


devices = braket.aws.device_search()

for device in devices:

    print(device.name)
```

2. **Submit Quantum Circuits to Hardware:** Once you've chosen a quantum device, submit your quantum circuit for execution on that hardware:

```python
Python


hardware_device = braket.aws.get_device(device_name="IonQ")

task = hardware_device.run(qc)

result = task.result()

print(result.measurements)
```

3. **Analyzing Results from Quantum Hardware:** When working with quantum hardware, you can retrieve the execution results and perform analysis. Note that quantum devices are subject to noise and imperfections, so results will include variances that require statistical analysis.

---

6. Optimizing Quantum Circuits for Hardware Execution

When designing quantum circuits for real hardware, certain factors should be taken into account to optimize performance and minimize errors:

- **Gate Fidelity:** High-fidelity gates are critical for ensuring reliable quantum operations.
- **Noise Mitigation:** Quantum devices are noisy by nature, so error correction techniques may be needed to improve the accuracy of results.

- **Resource Management:** Some quantum hardware platforms have limitations on the number of qubits or the depth of circuits, so optimization strategies are needed to fit algorithms within those limits.

The Braket SDK provides a robust environment for building, simulating, and executing quantum circuits, enabling quantum algorithm development for a wide range of applications. By integrating the SDK with quantum simulators and hardware backends, developers can create hybrid quantum-classical models, optimize quantum workflows, and explore the potential of quantum computing for machine learning, optimization, and beyond. Whether working with small-scale simulations or deploying large-scale tasks on real quantum hardware, Braket equips you with the tools needed for effective quantum programming and experimentation.

Integrating Quantum Machine Learning Workflows with Amazon Braket

Quantum Machine Learning (QML) represents a convergence of quantum computing and classical machine learning techniques, enabling novel computational approaches that harness the unique power of quantum systems. Amazon Braket, Amazon Web Services' (AWS) quantum computing service, provides a versatile and scalable platform for developing hybrid quantum-classical machine learning workflows. By combining the strengths of quantum computation with classical machine learning models, it is possible to achieve unprecedented efficiencies and solve complex tasks that are otherwise intractable for purely classical approaches.

This guide provides a high-level overview of how to integrate quantum machine learning workflows using Amazon Braket, focusing on building hybrid models, running variational algorithms, and training quantum circuits for machine learning tasks. The integration leverages Amazon Braket's rich ecosystem, which includes quantum simulators, hardware backends, and advanced algorithmic frameworks designed specifically for machine learning.

---

1. Understanding Quantum Machine Learning with Amazon Braket

Quantum Machine Learning combines quantum computing with classical machine learning models to leverage quantum resources, such as superposition, entanglement, and interference, in ways that classical models cannot. With quantum computing's potential for solving optimization problems, large-scale data analysis, and training more complex models, QML offers an exciting frontier for next-generation machine learning applications.

Amazon Braket offers various quantum simulators and hardware devices that support QML workflows. By using the Braket SDK, developers can implement variational algorithms and train quantum circuits, which are critical components of quantum machine learning models.

Key elements of QML workflows on Amazon Braket include:

- **Hybrid Quantum-Classical Models:** Combining classical machine learning models with quantum components, where quantum circuits are optimized based on classical data and vice versa.
- **Variational Algorithms:** Quantum circuits that are parameterized and can be trained using classical optimization techniques. These algorithms enable the integration of quantum resources into machine learning tasks.
- **Quantum Circuit Training:** Training quantum circuits to optimize parameters for tasks such as classification, regression, and optimization.

---

2. Setting Up a Hybrid Quantum-Classical Machine Learning Model

Building a hybrid quantum-classical model on Amazon Braket involves several key steps, where quantum operations complement classical machine learning processes. The main advantage of hybrid models is that they use classical machines to handle tasks that are well-suited to classical computation (such as data preprocessing) while using quantum computing for tasks that leverage quantum speed-ups (such as solving complex optimization problems).

Step 1: Define the Classical Machine Learning Component

First, select a classical machine learning algorithm that suits the problem at hand. Common classical models include support vector machines (SVMs), decision trees, or neural networks. In the hybrid setup, these classical models can provide an initial guess or baseline for the quantum circuit parameters.

For example, a typical classical model might involve:

- Preprocessing the dataset.
- Normalizing or scaling the features.
- Training a classical model to get preliminary results.

Step 2: Integrate Quantum Circuits into the Workflow

Once the classical model is defined, quantum components are introduced to handle specific aspects of the machine learning task. For instance, quantum circuits may be used to encode features, compute quantum-enhanced similarity measures, or solve optimization problems more efficiently.

Amazon Braket allows users to define quantum circuits using the `QuantumCircuit` class, providing a simple interface to create quantum gates and execute quantum operations. Here's a simple setup of a quantum circuit that encodes data into quantum states:

```
Python


from amazon_braket_sdk import QuantumCircuit


# Define quantum circuit with a single qubit

qc = QuantumCircuit(1)


# Apply Hadamard gate to put qubit in superposition

qc.h(0)
```

Step 3: Combine Classical and Quantum Optimization

Quantum circuits typically require optimization, which can be handled by classical optimization algorithms. For hybrid models, classical optimization techniques such as gradient descent or genetic algorithms can optimize quantum parameters in conjunction with the quantum circuit execution.

Using Amazon Braket's `HybridQuantumModel` class, users can integrate quantum operations into the training process of machine learning models. This process allows the quantum system to adapt its parameters in response to feedback from classical models:

```
Python
```

```
from amazon_braket_sdk import HybridQuantumModel


# Set up hybrid model by combining quantum and classical components

hybrid_model = HybridQuantumModel(quantum_circuit=qc,
classical_optimizer='gradient_descent')
```

---

3. Running Variational Algorithms for Machine Learning Tasks

Variational algorithms are a class of quantum algorithms that are particularly well-suited for quantum machine learning tasks. These algorithms involve parameterized quantum circuits whose parameters are optimized using classical techniques. They form the backbone of many quantum machine learning applications, such as variational quantum classifiers and quantum support vector machines (QSVM).

In Amazon Braket, variational algorithms can be implemented using parameterized quantum circuits. The `VQE` (Variational Quantum Eigensolver) or `QAOA` (Quantum Approximate Optimization Algorithm) can be applied to optimization problems, where quantum circuits are optimized with respect to classical inputs.

Step 1: Define the Quantum Circuit for Optimization

In the context of machine learning, the quantum circuit is typically a parameterized quantum circuit that encodes the data into quantum states, which are then manipulated to find the optimal solution for a given task. For example, consider a variational classifier circuit:

```
Python


from amazon_braket_sdk import QuantumCircuit


# Define a quantum circuit for classification task with two qubits

qc = QuantumCircuit(2)
```

```
# Apply quantum gates with tunable parameters

qc.rx(0, 'theta1')  # Apply rotation on qubit 0 with parameter theta1

qc.ry(1, 'theta2')  # Apply rotation on qubit 1 with parameter theta2
```

Step 2: Train the Quantum Circuit

The quantum circuit can now be trained by optimizing the parameters (`theta1`, `theta2`, etc.) using a classical optimizer, such as gradient descent. The optimizer adjusts the parameters based on the performance of the quantum circuit, which is evaluated using a cost function. This iterative process continues until an optimal solution is found.

```
Python


from amazon_braket_sdk import BraketOptimizer


# Use classical optimizer to optimize quantum circuit parameters

optimizer = BraketOptimizer()

optimized_circuit = optimizer.optimize(qc)
```

Step 3: Running the Variational Algorithm

Once the circuit is optimized, it can be run on a quantum simulator or a real quantum device to solve the machine learning task at hand, such as classification or regression. The output of the quantum circuit can be used as input to the classical machine learning component.

```
Python


# Execute the optimized quantum circuit on a simulator

result = simulator.run(optimized_circuit).result()
```

4. Training Quantum Circuits for Machine Learning Tasks

Training quantum circuits for machine learning tasks involves fine-tuning the quantum parameters based on feedback from the classical machine learning model. This requires the integration of quantum circuit execution within an iterative loop, similar to the training of classical models.

Step 1: Quantum Feature Mapping

One of the first steps in training quantum models is mapping classical data into quantum states, a process known as quantum feature mapping. Amazon Braket supports various methods for encoding classical data into quantum states, such as amplitude encoding, basis encoding, and angle encoding.

```
Python


from amazon_braket_sdk import QuantumCircuit


# Example: Encode classical data into quantum state

qc = QuantumCircuit(2)

qc.rx(0, 0.5)  # Encode classical feature as rotation angle
```

Step 2: Classical Optimization of Quantum Circuit

The quantum circuit is trained by adjusting its parameters to minimize a loss function. Classical optimization algorithms, such as stochastic gradient descent, are applied to the quantum circuit parameters to reduce the error in predictions.

```
Python


from amazon_braket_sdk import StochasticGradientDescent


# Initialize classical optimizer
```

```
optimizer = StochasticGradientDescent()


# Train quantum circuit

optimizer.train(qc, loss_function='mean_squared_error')
```

Step 3: Evaluating the Trained Model

After training the quantum circuit, evaluate its performance using test data. The evaluation step may involve measuring the circuit's output and comparing it with the ground truth for a given task. This is done by running the trained quantum circuit and analyzing the measurement results.

```
Python


result = qc.run()

print("Test Results:", result.measurements)
```

Integrating quantum machine learning workflows with Amazon Braket offers a promising approach for building hybrid models that combine quantum and classical computation to tackle some of the most challenging problems in machine learning. By utilizing Amazon Braket's flexible quantum simulators, hardware backends, and optimization tools, developers can efficiently design, test, and deploy quantum circuits that enhance classical machine learning algorithms. These hybrid models, powered by quantum circuits, can solve complex tasks in classification, regression, optimization, and beyond, paving the way for the future of quantum machine learning.

Practical Use Case: Deploying a Hybrid Quantum-Classical Model with Amazon Braket

In the ever-evolving field of Quantum Machine Learning (QML), hybrid quantum-classical models are emerging as powerful tools to solve real-world problems that classical computing alone cannot efficiently tackle. These models leverage the computational strengths of both quantum and classical systems to address challenges in areas like optimization, classification, and regression. Amazon Braket, AWS's quantum computing service, provides a seamless platform for developing and deploying such hybrid models, enabling businesses and researchers to harness the potential of quantum-enhanced machine learning workflows.

In this practical use case, we will guide you through the process of deploying a hybrid QML model using Amazon Braket, focusing on its application in a real-world problem, such as quantum-enhanced classification or regression. This process involves leveraging Amazon Braket's cloud-based quantum simulators, hardware backends, and classical optimization algorithms to create a robust hybrid system for machine learning tasks.

---

1. Overview of Hybrid Quantum-Classical Models

Hybrid quantum-classical models combine the efficiency of quantum computing for tasks that benefit from quantum acceleration (e.g., large-scale optimization or quantum feature mapping) with classical computing for tasks that are well-suited to traditional methods (e.g., data preprocessing, classical optimization). The core idea is that quantum resources are utilized where they offer a computational advantage, while classical models handle the bulk of the machine learning process.

In a typical hybrid quantum-classical model, the quantum circuit will be used to enhance specific aspects of the model, such as feature encoding or solving parts of an optimization problem, while the classical system manages the optimization loop, training, and model evaluation.

A hybrid quantum-classical model for classification or regression will typically involve the following components:

- **Quantum Circuit**: A parameterized quantum circuit that encodes the data and provides a quantum-enhanced feature map.
- **Classical Optimizer**: A classical optimization algorithm (e.g., gradient descent or other machine learning optimizers) that adjusts the quantum circuit's parameters.
- **Model Evaluation**: Classical methods for evaluating the model's performance on test data, including error metrics and validation.

Amazon Braket makes it easy to develop such models by offering a range of quantum simulators and hardware backends, as well as integration with classical machine learning workflows.

---

2. Setting Up the Environment in Amazon Braket

Before implementing and deploying a hybrid quantum-classical model, you first need to set up the appropriate environment in Amazon Braket, ensuring that you have access to quantum resources and tools for development.

Step 1: Configure Your Amazon Web Services (AWS) Account

To begin, ensure that you have an active AWS account and that you have set up Amazon Braket. This involves:

- Enabling Amazon Braket in your AWS account.
- Setting up IAM (Identity and Access Management) roles and permissions for quantum resources.
- Creating an S3 bucket to store quantum circuit data, training results, and logs.

```
Python


import boto3


# Create an AWS session for Amazon Braket

session = boto3.Session(profile_name='your-aws-profile')


# Create Amazon Braket client

braket_client = session.client('braket')
```

Step 2: Select Quantum Simulators or Hardware Backends

Amazon Braket provides access to both quantum simulators and actual quantum hardware backends. The choice between the two depends on the size and complexity of the quantum circuits, as well as the need for real quantum hardware in the experiment.

For initial testing and development, it's advisable to use a simulator. For production-level deployment or experiments requiring real quantum hardware, use the available quantum hardware backends from companies like Rigetti, IonQ, or D-Wave.

```
Python

# List available quantum simulators and hardware backends
backends = braket_client.list_quantum_backends()
```

---

3. Designing the Hybrid Quantum-Classical Model

Now, we can proceed with designing the hybrid quantum-classical model. The model involves creating a quantum circuit, encoding data, and integrating classical optimization methods to train the model.

Step 1: Define the Quantum Circuit

The quantum circuit is the heart of the quantum portion of the hybrid model. This parameterized circuit will encode classical data into quantum states, which can then be manipulated to extract quantum-enhanced information.

For example, in the case of a quantum-enhanced classification task, we might design a quantum circuit that uses a series of gates (such as Hadamard gates for superposition and Pauli-X or RX gates for rotations) to encode the data. Here's a basic example:

```
Python

from amazon_braket_sdk import QuantumCircuit

# Create a quantum circuit with two qubits
qc = QuantumCircuit(2)

# Apply quantum gates with tunable parameters for data encoding
qc.h(0)  # Hadamard gate to create superposition on qubit 0
qc.rx('theta1', 1)  # Parameterized rotation on qubit 1
```

```
qc.cx(0, 1)   # CNOT gate for entanglement
```

Step 2: Classical Optimization and Training

Once the quantum circuit is defined, we integrate a classical optimizer. This optimizer will adjust the parameters of the quantum circuit to minimize the model's loss function, such as mean squared error for regression or cross-entropy loss for classification.

For optimization, classical gradient-based methods such as stochastic gradient descent (SGD) or Adam are commonly used. Here's an example of how to integrate classical optimization with quantum circuit parameters:

```
Python


from amazon_braket_sdk import BraketOptimizer


# Define classical optimizer

optimizer = BraketOptimizer()


# Train the hybrid model with classical optimizer

optimized_parameters = optimizer.optimize(qc,
loss_function='mean_squared_error')
```

Step 3: Model Evaluation

Once the quantum circuit has been optimized, the next step is to evaluate the performance of the model on a test dataset. This evaluation can be done by running the quantum circuit and measuring the quantum states (e.g., using `measure` or `probability` functions) to extract results.

For instance, if the model is being used for classification, the output of the quantum circuit will be mapped to a specific class label, which can be compared against the true labels in the test set to compute accuracy.

```
Python
```

```
# Execute the optimized quantum circuit
result = braket_client.run_circuit(optimized_circuit).result()


# Measure the output of the quantum circuit
measurement = result.measurements
```

Step 4: Post-processing the Results

After obtaining the quantum circuit's results, post-processing steps are typically required. This involves interpreting the measurement results and mapping them back to the target output (e.g., class labels for classification or continuous values for regression).

For example, in a binary classification task, the quantum measurement results might be mapped to `0` or `1`:

```
Python


# Post-process measurement results for binary classification
class_predictions = [1 if outcome == '1' else 0 for outcome in
measurement]
```

---

4. Deploying the Hybrid Quantum-Classical Model

Once the model is developed and tested, it's time to deploy it for real-world use. The deployment process involves scaling the model, optimizing for speed and resource efficiency, and integrating it into production environments.

Step 1: Deploying the Model

To deploy the hybrid model, you can use AWS SageMaker for machine learning model deployment. Amazon SageMaker supports integrating quantum machine learning models into production pipelines, allowing seamless scaling and deployment of hybrid models.

```python
Python


import sagemaker

from sagemaker import get_execution_role


# Set up SageMaker for deployment

role = get_execution_role()

model = sagemaker.model.Model(

    image_uri='quantum-model-image-uri',

    role=role

)


# Deploy the model

predictor = model.deploy(initial_instance_count=1,
instance_type='ml.m5.large')
```

Step 2: Monitor and Optimize

Once deployed, it's critical to monitor the model's performance and optimize it as needed. AWS provides monitoring tools, such as CloudWatch, to track the usage and performance of deployed models, ensuring that they continue to meet the requirements of real-world applications.

Conclusion

By leveraging Amazon Braket's quantum computing resources, hybrid quantum-classical machine learning models can be implemented and deployed for real-world applications such as quantum-enhanced classification and regression. These models offer the potential to solve complex machine learning problems by exploiting the unique computational advantages of quantum systems, while still benefiting from the robustness and scalability of classical machine learning approaches.

With Amazon Braket's powerful suite of quantum simulators, hardware backends, and classical optimization tools, developers can efficiently build, optimize, and deploy hybrid models that have the potential to revolutionize industries ranging from finance to healthcare to logistics. The deployment of such models marks a significant step toward the future of machine learning in the quantum age.

PART 3: Implementing Quantum Machine Learning Solutions

Part 3: Implementing Quantum Machine Learning Solutions focuses on applying quantum machine learning concepts to real-world problems and developing practical solutions. Readers will learn how to design and implement quantum algorithms, such as variational quantum classifiers and quantum-enhanced optimization models, to address complex tasks. Through industry-driven case studies, this section demonstrates the application of quantum machine learning in fields like finance, healthcare, logistics, and AI, showcasing its potential to solve problems beyond the reach of classical methods. Additionally, readers will explore benchmarks and comparisons between classical and quantum approaches, gaining insight into the advantages, limitations, and performance of quantum models. By the end of this part, readers will be equipped to tackle real-world challenges using quantum machine learning and integrate these solutions into modern workflows.

CHAPTER 8: Designing Quantum Algorithms for Machine Learning

DESCRIPTION:

This chapter focuses on the **design and implementation of quantum algorithms** tailored for machine learning tasks. Readers will explore key quantum algorithms, such as the Quantum Fourier Transform, Quantum Principal Component Analysis, and Variational Quantum Algorithms, and understand how they can solve machine learning problems more efficiently. Through hands-on examples and explanations, this chapter bridges theoretical quantum concepts and their practical applications in machine learning.

Introduction to Quantum Algorithms for Machine Learning

Quantum algorithms represent a transformative approach to solving computational problems that are intractable or inefficient for classical computers. With quantum mechanics harnessed to process and analyze data, quantum algorithms promise substantial advancements in machine learning (ML), particularly for tasks involving large datasets, high-dimensional spaces, and complex optimization problems. This section introduces the foundational concepts of quantum algorithms for machine learning (QML), explores their role in enhancing ML workflows, and provides a deeper understanding of their potential advantages over traditional methods.

The Role of Quantum Algorithms in Machine Learning

In classical machine learning, algorithms are designed to analyze data, identify patterns, and make predictions or decisions based on statistical models and computational techniques. However, as the complexity of data increases—such as in high-dimensional feature spaces or large datasets—the computational burden on classical systems grows, often leading to inefficiency, long processing times, and difficulties in scaling.

Quantum computing offers a potential breakthrough by leveraging quantum bits (qubits) that can exist in multiple states simultaneously, thanks to the principles of superposition and entanglement. This ability to process an exponentially larger number of possibilities in parallel gives quantum algorithms a unique advantage in performing complex calculations much more efficiently than classical algorithms in certain contexts.

Quantum machine learning algorithms aim to exploit these quantum phenomena to perform faster computations, higher-dimensional data analysis, and more effective optimization techniques. By doing so, QML can help overcome some of the inherent limitations of classical machine learning, such as issues with scaling, convergence speed, and accuracy in optimization tasks.

Quantum Speed-Up: The Power of Quantum Algorithms

One of the key benefits of quantum algorithms in machine learning is their potential to provide quantum speed-up. Quantum speed-up refers to the ability of quantum computers to solve specific problems significantly faster than classical computers. This occurs due to quantum properties like superposition, entanglement, and interference, which allow quantum computers to process information in a parallel manner that classical systems cannot replicate.

For instance, tasks like matrix inversion, feature space mapping, and solving linear systems—core operations in machine learning—can be exponentially more efficient on quantum hardware compared to classical approaches. Quantum algorithms such as **Quantum Singular Value Decomposition (QSVD)** and **Quantum Principal Component Analysis (QPCA)** promise to perform dimensionality reduction and data encoding much faster than classical counterparts. This reduction in time complexity could enable faster training of machine learning models, particularly for large-scale datasets.

Moreover, quantum speed-up can drastically reduce the time required for optimization problems in ML tasks, such as training deep neural networks, hyperparameter tuning, and solving complex nonlinear problems. In such cases, quantum algorithms can provide solutions in polynomial time where classical methods may take exponential time.

Hybrid Quantum-Classical Approaches: Combining the Best of Both Worlds

While quantum algorithms hold great promise, the current state of quantum hardware and algorithms is still in its nascent stages. Quantum systems have limited qubits, noise, and error rates, which makes them unsuitable for solving all machine learning problems on their own at scale. This is where **hybrid quantum-classical approaches** become vital.

Hybrid quantum-classical models combine the strengths of both quantum and classical computing. In these models, quantum algorithms are used for specific components of the ML pipeline, particularly those that benefit most from quantum speed-up, while classical algorithms handle other components, such as data preprocessing, error correction, or final decision-making.

A common hybrid approach involves using **variational quantum algorithms**, such as the **Variational Quantum Eigensolver (VQE)** or **Quantum Approximate Optimization Algorithm (QAOA)**, where quantum circuits are used to optimize certain aspects of the model (e.g., training a model), while classical computers are used to control the optimization process. This allows quantum algorithms to solve subproblems (like parameter optimization) more efficiently, while the classical system handles the broader task.

For example, in a hybrid quantum-classical neural network (QNN), a quantum circuit could be used to encode input data or perform feature mapping, while the classical side trains the network, adjusts weights, and performs final predictions. This combination allows quantum algorithms to enhance specific steps of the machine learning process, delivering an overall more efficient model.

Key Concepts in Quantum Machine Learning Algorithms

- **Quantum Data Representation**: Quantum algorithms often rely on **quantum states** to represent data. By encoding data in quantum systems, algorithms can leverage quantum parallelism to process multiple data points simultaneously. Quantum data representation is key for efficiently tackling high-dimensional and complex datasets.
- **Quantum-enhanced Optimization**: Many ML algorithms rely on optimization techniques to minimize loss functions or maximize performance metrics. Quantum algorithms can provide quantum-enhanced optimization methods, such as **Quantum Gradient Descent** and **Quantum Annealing**, which can outperform classical optimization methods by exploring vast solution spaces more effectively.
- **Quantum State Preparation**: Quantum algorithms for ML often begin with **quantum state preparation**, where classical data is encoded into quantum states. This is typically done using quantum feature maps or by directly encoding the classical data into the quantum system. The choice of encoding method significantly impacts the efficiency of the quantum algorithm.
- **Quantum Circuit Design**: Quantum circuits are the heart of quantum machine learning algorithms. These circuits are designed to process quantum data, perform operations on it (such as gates, entanglements, or measurements), and extract useful information. Designing efficient quantum circuits is key to harnessing quantum advantages.

Applications of Quantum Algorithms in Machine Learning

Quantum algorithms can be applied across various machine learning tasks, from classification to clustering, and even in more advanced areas like reinforcement learning and deep learning.

- **Quantum Support Vector Machines (QSVM)**: This quantum enhancement of classical SVMs allows for faster classification in high-dimensional spaces by exploiting quantum parallelism to process large feature sets more efficiently.
- **Quantum k-Means Clustering**: By applying quantum algorithms to clustering tasks, it becomes possible to analyze large datasets and uncover hidden patterns with greater speed and accuracy.

- **Quantum Principal Component Analysis (QPCA)**: QPCA can perform dimensionality reduction on quantum hardware, processing data more efficiently in high-dimensional spaces, and allowing for faster learning tasks in real-world scenarios.
- **Quantum Neural Networks (QNN)**: Hybrid quantum-classical neural networks leverage quantum circuits to perform computations more efficiently in tasks like pattern recognition, optimization, and function approximation.

Quantum algorithms are positioned to revolutionize machine learning by offering computational advantages that are not achievable with classical computing alone. By exploiting quantum properties like superposition, entanglement, and interference, these algorithms promise speed-up, efficiency, and scalability in tasks such as classification, optimization, and clustering. However, due to current hardware limitations, the most effective way to leverage quantum machine learning is through hybrid approaches, combining the power of quantum and classical systems to deliver optimized results. As quantum hardware improves and algorithms evolve, the role of quantum algorithms in machine learning will continue to expand, unlocking new possibilities for industries ranging from healthcare to finance and beyond.

Quantum Fourier Transform (QFT) and Its Applications in Machine Learning

The Quantum Fourier Transform (QFT) is a cornerstone of many quantum algorithms, offering a quantum-enhanced counterpart to the classical Fourier Transform. In classical computing, the Fourier Transform plays a crucial role in signal processing, data compression, and frequency analysis by transforming signals from the time domain into the frequency domain. The QFT, leveraging quantum superposition and parallelism, provides significant speed-ups for certain types of computations, particularly when dealing with complex, high-dimensional data.

In the context of quantum machine learning (QML), the QFT enables several transformative techniques, from data encoding to feature extraction. Understanding its mechanics, and how to implement and integrate it into machine learning workflows, is vital for developing quantum-enhanced algorithms that outperform their classical counterparts. This section delves into the quantum Fourier transform, its practical applications, and its powerful implications for quantum machine learning tasks.

What is the Quantum Fourier Transform (QFT)?

The Quantum Fourier Transform is the quantum analog of the classical discrete Fourier transform (DFT). Like the DFT, the QFT operates on discrete data, but unlike the classical DFT, it can process multiple data points simultaneously, thanks to quantum parallelism. The key difference lies in the fact that quantum operations, like superposition and entanglement, allow the QFT to compute the Fourier coefficients in a quantum system exponentially faster than classical systems for certain problem sets.

Mathematically, the QFT acts on quantum bits (qubits) to transform an input state into its Fourier-transformed state. Given a quantum state $|x\rangle$, the QFT maps this state into another state $|\tilde{x}\rangle$ that represents the Fourier-transformed version. The transformation is implemented via a series of quantum gates, including Hadamard gates and controlled phase gates, operating in a way that can exploit quantum parallelism.

In terms of its computational complexity, the QFT provides an exponential speed-up in the number of operations compared to its classical counterpart, reducing the time complexity of transforming a quantum state from $O(N^2)$ in classical Fourier transforms to $O(N \log N)$ in QFT. This efficiency allows quantum computers to handle large data sets in a fraction of the time it would take a classical computer.

Implementation of the Quantum Fourier Transform

Implementing the QFT on quantum hardware requires constructing a quantum circuit using basic quantum gates that apply transformations to the qubits. These transformations manipulate the quantum state according to the rules of quantum mechanics, allowing for parallel computation.

The steps to implement the QFT on n qubits are as follows:

1. **Initialization**: Begin with an n −qubit quantum state, usually set to $|0\rangle$.
2. **Hadamard Transform**: Apply a Hadamard gate to the first qubit. This creates an equal superposition of states, enabling the necessary quantum parallelism.
3. **Controlled Phase Rotations**: Sequentially apply controlled phase gates. Each phase gate is conditioned on the previous qubit's state, introducing a specific phase shift depending on the bit positions.
4. **Reverse Qubits**: After performing the Hadamard and controlled phase gates, reverse the order of the qubits to achieve the final transformed state. This reversal is a key difference between the QFT and the classical Fourier transform.

5. **Measurement**: Once the QFT has been applied, measurement of the quantum state will provide the Fourier-transformed data.

By leveraging the quantum properties of superposition and entanglement, the QFT can efficiently perform these operations in parallel, reducing the overall complexity.

Applications of the Quantum Fourier Transform in Machine Learning

The Quantum Fourier Transform holds significant promise for a range of quantum machine learning applications. It is particularly valuable in problems that require high-dimensional data manipulation, data encoding, feature extraction, and solving optimization problems that benefit from quantum speed-ups.

1. Data Encoding

Quantum data encoding involves converting classical data into a quantum state that can be processed using quantum algorithms. The QFT plays a pivotal role in this process, as it allows for efficient mapping of classical data into quantum states that can be operated on by other quantum algorithms.

For example, in quantum machine learning models, data encoding schemes such as **quantum amplitude encoding** or **quantum feature mapping** benefit from the QFT's ability to map data into high-dimensional quantum states. This provides a compact and highly efficient representation of classical data that can then be manipulated within a quantum computer's quantum parallelism.

By performing a QFT, we can exploit the full potential of quantum state representations, enabling faster computations and providing a deeper understanding of the intrinsic structure of the data, essential for training models in quantum machine learning.

2. Feature Extraction

Feature extraction in machine learning involves identifying the most relevant features from a large dataset, reducing its dimensionality and improving the performance of machine learning algorithms. The QFT can be applied to accelerate this process, especially when dealing with periodic or oscillatory patterns within data.

In classical machine learning, techniques like Fourier transforms help in identifying dominant frequency components within signals, a process known as **frequency domain analysis**. In quantum machine learning, the QFT can be applied directly to data encoded into quantum states, revealing essential features like frequencies and correlations that might otherwise be computationally expensive or even infeasible to compute with classical systems.

For example, when using quantum circuits for feature extraction, the QFT can be employed to identify hidden periodicities or oscillatory patterns within the data—useful in time-series analysis, signal processing, and other domains. This makes QFT an essential tool for developing quantum-enhanced feature extraction techniques, particularly in complex datasets with underlying periodic or repetitive structures.

3. Quantum-enhanced Optimization

In optimization problems—whether they involve training machine learning models, fine-tuning hyperparameters, or solving combinatorial optimization tasks—quantum algorithms have the potential to offer significant speed-ups. The QFT can aid in quantum-enhanced optimization by efficiently exploring high-dimensional solution spaces.

For instance, in tasks like **quantum approximate optimization** or **variational quantum eigensolvers**, the QFT can be used to represent the problem's solution space in a more compact, high-dimensional quantum state. This enables quantum circuits to explore more potential solutions simultaneously and can result in faster convergence and higher-quality solutions for optimization problems compared to classical methods.

4. Quantum Signal Processing and Classification

In tasks such as classification, the QFT can assist in transforming and analyzing quantum data to identify patterns or features that are critical for accurate predictions. Quantum signal processing, which typically involves analyzing signals for noise reduction, feature extraction, and transformation, is an area where the QFT can significantly reduce the complexity and time required for these operations.

For example, quantum algorithms such as **Quantum Support Vector Machines (QSVM)** or **Quantum Neural Networks (QNN)** can leverage the QFT to map quantum data into a form that is suitable for efficient learning. By using the QFT to extract relevant features, these models can achieve improved accuracy and faster training times.

The Quantum Fourier Transform is an indispensable tool in the quantum computing and machine learning toolkit, offering significant advantages for data encoding, feature extraction, optimization, and signal processing. By efficiently transforming quantum states, the QFT enables quantum machine learning algorithms to process high-dimensional data faster and more effectively than classical counterparts. As quantum hardware continues to advance, the applications of the QFT in machine learning will expand, offering new ways to solve complex, large-scale problems across a variety of industries. Understanding and implementing the QFT is a crucial step toward unlocking the full potential of quantum-enhanced machine learning.

Quantum Principal Component Analysis (qPCA)

Quantum Principal Component Analysis (qPCA) represents a quantum-enhanced approach to Principal Component Analysis (PCA), one of the most fundamental and widely used techniques in classical machine learning and data science for dimensionality reduction. The classical PCA algorithm operates by transforming high-dimensional data into a lower-dimensional space, preserving as much of the variance (information) as possible. It achieves this by identifying the principal components—directions of maximum variance in the data—via eigenvalue decomposition of the data's covariance matrix.

While PCA is efficient for many problems, it becomes computationally expensive for large datasets, particularly when the dataset's dimensionality is extremely high. Quantum computing, leveraging principles like superposition, entanglement, and quantum parallelism, can dramatically accelerate PCA through a quantum variant—quantum PCA (qPCA). The key advantage of qPCA lies in its potential to process data in exponentially faster time than classical PCA, especially when dealing with large, high-dimensional datasets.

In this section, we will explore the design and application of the qPCA algorithm, explain its use in dimensionality reduction, and understand how it addresses challenges inherent in classical PCA, particularly in the context of quantum-enhanced machine learning workflows.

What is Quantum Principal Component Analysis (qPCA)?

Quantum Principal Component Analysis (qPCA) leverages quantum algorithms to extract principal components from a dataset more efficiently than classical algorithms. The qPCA algorithm computes the principal eigenvectors and eigenvalues of the data covariance matrix, which is the core process in classical PCA. However, qPCA uses quantum operations to perform these calculations, potentially offering exponential speed-ups.

Unlike classical PCA, which involves the expensive process of diagonalizing the covariance matrix (an operation that takes $O(d^3)$ time for a dataset of d dimensions), qPCA uses quantum computers to perform this operation in a much faster and more efficient manner. This is made possible by exploiting quantum properties like superposition and interference to represent the dataset in a quantum state, and then applying quantum algorithms such as the **quantum phase estimation algorithm** or **quantum singular value estimation**.

The quantum algorithm for qPCA does not require the explicit calculation of the covariance matrix. Instead, it operates directly on the quantum state representing the data, which can lead to exponential reductions in the computational resources required.

The qPCA Algorithm Design

The quantum principal component analysis algorithm typically consists of the following key steps:

1. **Data Representation**:
    - In qPCA, the first step is to represent the classical dataset in a quantum format. One common method is **quantum state preparation**, where the classical data is encoded into a quantum state, typically using techniques like **amplitude encoding** or **quantum feature mapping**.
    - In amplitude encoding, each classical data point is mapped to a quantum amplitude, where the quantum state $|\psi\rangle$ represents the data in a superposition of basis states.
2. **Quantum Phase Estimation**:
    - Quantum phase estimation is one of the key quantum algorithms used in qPCA to extract the eigenvalues and eigenvectors of a matrix, which in this case is the covariance matrix of the dataset.
    - This algorithm allows the quantum system to efficiently estimate the eigenvalues of the data's covariance matrix, which represent the variance of the data along each principal component direction.
3. **Quantum Singular Value Decomposition (SVD)**:
    - Singular value decomposition (SVD) is a generalization of the eigenvalue decomposition and plays a critical role in dimensionality reduction tasks, such as PCA. In qPCA, quantum singular value decomposition is performed to compute the principal components (the eigenvectors) corresponding to the largest singular values.
    - SVD on quantum computers can be performed exponentially faster than on classical computers. Algorithms like **quantum singular value estimation** can be

used to efficiently compute the singular values, reducing the time complexity of the problem.

4. **Eigenvector Calculation**:
    - Once the eigenvalues have been obtained via quantum phase estimation, the corresponding eigenvectors can be extracted by using quantum operations such as **quantum amplitude estimation**. This step is crucial as the eigenvectors represent the principal components of the data.
    - The quantum state evolves in such a way that these eigenvectors are computed in parallel, enabling an exponential speed-up.
5. **Dimensionality Reduction**:
    - Once the eigenvectors are obtained, qPCA can project the high-dimensional data onto a lower-dimensional subspace. This step, like classical PCA, reduces the number of features while preserving the most significant components of the dataset.
    - The dimensionality reduction process in qPCA involves measuring the quantum state to collapse it into the subspace spanned by the top principal components.

Applications of qPCA in Machine Learning

Quantum PCA offers promising advantages in machine learning, particularly for tasks that involve large datasets or high-dimensional data where classical PCA struggles. Some of the most compelling applications of qPCA include:

1. High-Dimensional Data Processing

As datasets become increasingly large and high-dimensional, classical PCA can become slow and computationally expensive. For large datasets with millions of features, qPCA can efficiently handle the data by processing it in a quantum state, reducing both time complexity and memory requirements. This makes qPCA particularly valuable in fields such as genomics, neuroscience, and high-energy physics, where high-dimensional data is ubiquitous.

2. Speeding Up Dimensionality Reduction

Dimensionality reduction is a core task in many machine learning workflows, where reducing the number of features while maintaining data variance can significantly improve model performance. qPCA accelerates the dimensionality reduction process, making it possible to handle datasets that are too large or complex for classical algorithms.

For instance, in applications like image recognition or natural language processing (NLP), where data dimensionality can be in the thousands or millions of features, qPCA can provide a quantum-enhanced solution for reducing the number of features required, making it easier to train machine learning models.

3. Quantum Data Compression

qPCA can be applied in quantum data compression tasks. By using quantum algorithms to identify the principal components of large datasets, qPCA can reduce the dataset's size while maintaining the key features for analysis. This is particularly useful for quantum machine learning models, which often need to work with large datasets stored in quantum states.

4. Quantum-Enhanced Clustering

Clustering tasks, such as k-means or hierarchical clustering, benefit from dimensionality reduction techniques like PCA. qPCA can improve the clustering process by reducing the number of dimensions, leading to faster and more efficient clustering algorithms. The reduced data space also allows for better identification of inherent patterns within the data, improving the overall clustering performance.

5. Quantum Classification

In supervised learning, dimensionality reduction through qPCA can also be used to preprocess data before classification. By extracting the most significant features from the data, qPCA can improve the accuracy and performance of quantum classifiers such as Quantum Support Vector Machines (QSVMs) or Quantum Neural Networks (QNNs). The reduced feature set allows the quantum classifier to operate more efficiently, resulting in faster training and better generalization.

Challenges and Limitations

Despite its potential, qPCA is still in the early stages of development, and several challenges need to be addressed before it can be widely applied:

- **Quantum Hardware Limitations**: Current quantum hardware is still in its nascent stages, with qubits prone to noise and decoherence. Implementing qPCA on noisy intermediate-scale quantum (NISQ) devices may result in inaccuracies or limitations in the size of the datasets that can be processed.

- **Quantum State Preparation**: Efficiently encoding large classical datasets into quantum states is a non-trivial task. The complexity of quantum state preparation may limit the practical applicability of qPCA on very large datasets.
- **Error Correction**: Quantum error correction techniques will be critical for ensuring that qPCA algorithms work reliably on noisy quantum systems. The development of fault-tolerant quantum computing will likely be necessary to fully unlock the potential of qPCA.

Quantum Principal Component Analysis (qPCA) offers a quantum-enhanced approach to one of the most widely used techniques in classical machine learning: dimensionality reduction. By exploiting quantum properties such as superposition and parallelism, qPCA can potentially revolutionize how we process and analyze large, high-dimensional datasets. While challenges remain in terms of quantum hardware capabilities and error correction, the ability to handle large datasets more efficiently with qPCA will play a crucial role in the evolution of quantum machine learning and its applications across industries such as healthcare, finance, and beyond. As quantum hardware continues to improve, qPCA is poised to become an essential tool for future machine learning workflows.

Variational Quantum Algorithms (VQAs)

Variational Quantum Algorithms (VQAs) represent a class of quantum algorithms that leverage both quantum and classical resources to solve complex computational problems, with particular emphasis on optimization tasks commonly encountered in machine learning, chemistry, and other fields. The core idea behind VQAs is to combine quantum circuits with classical optimization techniques to iteratively minimize a cost function, which is typically a function of the quantum state that encodes the solution to a given problem.

VQAs are particularly significant for near-term quantum computers, where large-scale quantum operations (such as Shor's algorithm) are still impractical due to the limited number of qubits and quantum gate fidelity. Instead, VQAs operate within the noisy, intermediate-scale quantum (NISQ) era, taking advantage of quantum parallelism and quantum gates to perform hybrid computations, with the classical component handling optimization and feedback loops.

In this section, we will delve into the design, implementation, and application of two of the most prominent VQAs—**Variational Quantum Eigensolver (VQE)** and **Quantum Approximate Optimization Algorithm (QAOA)**—which have found widespread application in solving optimization problems within machine learning and other fields.

What Are Variational Quantum Algorithms (VQAs)?

Variational Quantum Algorithms are iterative algorithms that combine quantum circuits to prepare quantum states with classical optimization methods to tune the parameters of the quantum circuit. They are used to solve problems for which the optimal solution can be represented as the ground state of a Hamiltonian or to optimize a classical objective function using quantum resources.

VQAs involve two main components:

1. **Quantum Circuit**: A parameterized quantum circuit that evolves through a sequence of quantum gates, preparing a quantum state that encodes the solution.
2. **Classical Optimization Loop**: An external classical optimizer that adjusts the parameters of the quantum circuit iteratively to minimize (or maximize) a cost function, which is usually a measure of the quantum state's quality or the problem's objective.

VQAs are considered particularly useful for problems where the quantum advantage lies in the efficient handling of high-dimensional spaces that are too complex for classical methods, especially for large datasets in machine learning, chemical simulation, and optimization tasks.

Key Variational Quantum Algorithms

1. **Variational Quantum Eigensolver (VQE)**

The **Variational Quantum Eigensolver (VQE)** is one of the most well-known VQAs, specifically designed to find the eigenvalues and eigenvectors of a Hamiltonian—a mathematical representation of the energy states of a system. In machine learning, VQE has been applied to quantum chemistry simulations, where finding the ground state energy of a molecule's Hamiltonian is a key task. In this context, the VQE algorithm is used to compute the lowest energy configuration (or ground state) of a quantum system, which is analogous to solving optimization problems in machine learning by searching for the best state or model.

VQE Algorithm Design:

1. **Initial State Preparation**: The quantum circuit starts with a known initial state, typically a simple quantum state like $|0\rangle$ or a state chosen based on the problem domain.

2. **Parameterized Quantum Circuit**: A series of quantum gates are applied to the quantum state, where each gate has tunable parameters. This creates a family of quantum states that can be adjusted by varying the parameters.
3. **Measurement and Classical Optimization**: The quantum state is measured, and the expectation value of the Hamiltonian is computed, which is the cost function. The classical optimizer then adjusts the parameters of the quantum circuit to minimize the expectation value, iterating until convergence to the ground state.

Applications of VQE:

- **Quantum Chemistry**: VQE has been applied to compute the ground state energy of molecules, which is a crucial task in simulating quantum chemical systems.
- **Machine Learning**: VQE can be used to optimize variational parameters in quantum machine learning models, where the aim is to find the best quantum representation of data or model parameters.
- **Optimization**: The VQE approach is used in optimization tasks such as finding the minimal configuration of energy or resource allocation problems.

2. **Quantum Approximate Optimization Algorithm (QAOA)**

The **Quantum Approximate Optimization Algorithm (QAOA)** is another important VQA that is specifically designed to solve combinatorial optimization problems. Unlike VQE, which is used to solve problems related to finding eigenvalues, QAOA is focused on solving discrete optimization problems, particularly those that can be formulated as Max-Cut problems or other combinatorial problems in machine learning and optimization domains.

QAOA Algorithm Design:

1. **Problem Mapping**: The first step in QAOA is to map the optimization problem into a Hamiltonian, where the goal is to find the ground state or low-energy states of this Hamiltonian.
2. **Parameterized Quantum Circuit**: A quantum circuit with a series of parameterized gates is used to prepare a quantum state. The parameters of these gates are adjusted to create a state that is as close as possible to the optimal solution of the problem.
3. **Quantum Measurement**: After running the quantum circuit, the quantum state is measured, and the corresponding objective function (or cost function) is evaluated.

4. **Classical Optimization**: The classical optimizer then updates the parameters based on the measured cost function and repeats the process iteratively to converge to the optimal solution.

Applications of QAOA:

- **Combinatorial Optimization**: QAOA has found significant applications in solving problems such as Max-Cut, which is a common problem in machine learning and computer science that involves dividing a graph into two parts while minimizing the weight of edges between the parts.
- **Machine Learning**: In machine learning, QAOA can be used for optimization tasks such as feature selection, model selection, or solving linear programming problems in constrained optimization.
- **Quantum Circuits Design**: QAOA has been applied to optimize the design of quantum circuits themselves, helping to minimize the resource usage in large-scale quantum computations.

Building and Training VQAs

Building and training VQAs for machine learning tasks involves creating quantum circuits that are parameterized for optimization problems and integrating them into hybrid quantum-classical frameworks. Here's a step-by-step breakdown of how to build and train VQAs like VQE and QAOA:

1. **Define the Problem**: Start by clearly defining the problem that needs to be optimized. For VQE, this would involve identifying the Hamiltonian representing the energy states of a quantum system, whereas for QAOA, the problem would typically involve encoding a combinatorial optimization task (e.g., Max-Cut).
2. **Quantum Circuit Design**:
   - For VQE, design a parameterized quantum circuit that prepares a quantum state capable of representing the problem's solution.
   - For QAOA, construct the quantum circuit based on the problem's Hamiltonian, applying alternating layers of problem-specific and mixing Hamiltonians to generate states that can represent various solutions.
3. **Hybrid Quantum-Classical Optimization Loop**:

- The quantum circuit is executed multiple times with varying parameters, and the outcome of each execution is measured. The classical optimizer uses the results to update the quantum circuit's parameters, iterating until convergence.
- Classical optimization methods such as gradient descent, conjugate gradient methods, or evolutionary algorithms are typically used to optimize the quantum parameters.

4. **Training the Algorithm**:
   - Train the variational quantum model by repeatedly adjusting the quantum circuit's parameters through the optimization loop. Use the measured outcomes (such as the expectation value of the Hamiltonian in VQE or the cost function in QAOA) to evaluate the performance of the current set of parameters.
   - Monitor convergence over iterations and ensure that the optimizer converges to the optimal parameters corresponding to the best solution.
5. **Evaluation and Performance**:
   - After the optimization loop completes, evaluate the performance of the quantum-enhanced model by testing its ability to solve the original problem.
   - In machine learning, evaluate how the optimized model generalizes on new, unseen data.

Advantages and Challenges of VQAs

Advantages:

- **Quantum Speedup**: VQAs offer potential quantum speedups for specific optimization problems, particularly in high-dimensional and complex spaces where classical algorithms may struggle.
- **Hybrid Efficiency**: VQAs combine the strengths of quantum and classical computation, taking advantage of quantum's ability to handle complex systems while leveraging classical optimization methods for parameter tuning.
- **Broad Applicability**: VQAs are adaptable to a wide range of problems in machine learning, quantum chemistry, and combinatorial optimization, making them versatile for many real-world applications.

Challenges:

- **Quantum Hardware Limitations**: The effectiveness of VQAs depends on the availability of quantum hardware with sufficient qubits and low noise. NISQ devices are prone to errors, which can limit the accuracy of results.
- **Optimization Challenges**: The classical optimization loop for VQAs can be computationally expensive, particularly for complex problems where many iterations may be required.
- **Noise and Decoherence**: Quantum systems are susceptible to noise and decoherence, which can affect the precision of quantum measurements and hinder the performance of the VQA.

Variational Quantum Algorithms (VQAs) like Variational Quantum Eigensolver (VQE) and Quantum Approximate Optimization Algorithm (QAOA) offer transformative approaches to solving complex optimization problems. By combining quantum computing's power to handle high-dimensional spaces with classical optimization techniques, VQAs hold great promise for solving real-world problems in machine learning, combinatorial optimization, quantum chemistry, and more.

As quantum hardware continues to evolve, the efficiency of VQAs will improve, making them an indispensable tool in the quantum machine learning toolkit. By understanding the fundamental principles and practical applications of VQAs, researchers and practitioners can harness the full potential of quantum computing to tackle some of the most challenging problems in various domains.

Practical Use Case: Designing a Custom Quantum Algorithm for Machine Learning

In the ever-evolving intersection of quantum computing and machine learning, the integration of quantum algorithms offers transformative possibilities for tackling some of the most complex problems in modern data science. A custom quantum machine learning (QML) solution, tailored to a specific real-world problem such as clustering or classification, can leverage quantum parallelism, speedup, and high-dimensional state spaces to solve problems that are intractable for classical algorithms.

This practical use case explores how quantum algorithms can be combined and customized to create a robust and efficient quantum machine learning solution. The goal is to design a quantum algorithm that solves a machine learning task—in this case, clustering or classification—that takes full advantage of quantum resources to outperform classical approaches.

Defining the Problem: Quantum Clustering or Classification

In machine learning, clustering and classification are fundamental tasks:

1. **Clustering**: The goal of clustering is to partition a dataset into groups based on similarities in the data. Classical algorithms like k-means and hierarchical clustering typically perform well for smaller datasets but can struggle with high-dimensional, noisy, or complex datasets.
2. **Classification**: Classification involves predicting a label for each input based on learned patterns. Classical machine learning models, such as support vector machines (SVMs) or decision trees, can face limitations in terms of computational efficiency and scalability when dealing with large or complex datasets.

For these tasks, a custom quantum machine learning solution can combine existing quantum algorithms (such as the Quantum Support Vector Machine (QSVM), Quantum k-means, or Quantum Principal Component Analysis (qPCA)) with tailored quantum circuits, providing potential speedups and enhanced accuracy.

Designing the Quantum Machine Learning Solution

Step 1: Quantum Data Encoding

Quantum machine learning algorithms rely on encoding classical data into quantum states. This step is critical because quantum states have the potential to represent exponentially large datasets using only a few qubits, a property known as **quantum parallelism**.

For clustering or classification tasks, the input data must be mapped into a quantum space, typically using one of the following methods:

- **Amplitude Encoding**: Classical data is encoded into the amplitudes of quantum states. For a dataset with N features, amplitude encoding represents the data in a high-dimensional quantum state, allowing quantum algorithms to explore exponentially larger spaces than classical algorithms.
- **Basis Encoding**: This encoding method represents each data point as a basis state of a quantum system. Although less efficient than amplitude encoding, it is sometimes used when dealing with small datasets or low-dimensional feature spaces.

- **Angle Encoding**: Another approach involves mapping the data to the angles of quantum gates. Angle encoding is particularly useful for parameterized quantum circuits, where the data points influence the rotation angles of quantum gates.

For clustering, the quantum data encoding should be designed to represent the distance or similarity between data points in a high-dimensional quantum space. For classification, the encoding should capture the class information and map it to a quantum state.

Step 2: Custom Quantum Circuit Design

With the data encoded in quantum states, the next step is to design a quantum circuit capable of performing the desired machine learning task. This involves selecting or designing quantum algorithms that exploit quantum advantages for clustering or classification.

1. **Quantum Clustering**: Quantum k-means clustering is a natural candidate for clustering tasks. The classical k-means algorithm relies on iteratively updating centroids and reassigning data points based on distance measures. Quantum k-means leverages quantum parallelism to compute distances in a superposition of quantum states, which allows for exponentially faster processing of large datasets.
    - **Quantum k-means Algorithm**:
        - Prepare quantum states that encode the data points.
        - Use quantum gates to calculate the distance between each data point and the centroids, typically by using quantum circuits that encode pairwise distance measures (e.g., the Hamming distance between quantum states or inner product measures).
        - Use quantum measurement to select the closest centroids.
        - Iterate the process, updating centroids and reassigning points, using a quantum-classical feedback loop.

    This quantum clustering algorithm is faster and more scalable than classical k-means, especially when applied to high-dimensional datasets.

2. **Quantum Classification**: Quantum algorithms for classification tasks, such as the Quantum Support Vector Machine (QSVM), can be customized for specific problems. The quantum version of SVM leverages the quantum kernel trick, which

maps the data to a high-dimensional quantum space, where linear separability is more likely to occur.

- **Quantum Support Vector Machine (QSVM)**:
  - Encode the data into quantum states, using a suitable quantum feature map (kernel).
  - Use a quantum processor to compute the inner products between data points in the feature space, which is more efficient than classical computations.
  - Train the classifier by minimizing the classification error using quantum algorithms, typically employing a quantum optimization method like the Variational Quantum Eigensolver (VQE).

The QSVM provides quantum speedup for certain datasets, particularly in cases where the data is linearly separable in high-dimensional quantum feature spaces but not in classical space.

Step 3: Hybrid Quantum-Classical Optimization

To improve the efficiency and scalability of quantum machine learning algorithms, a hybrid quantum-classical optimization approach can be employed. This combines the power of quantum circuits with classical optimization techniques to adjust the quantum parameters iteratively.

- **Quantum-Classical Feedback Loop**: In this loop, the quantum circuit generates a quantum state that encodes the solution (e.g., cluster assignments or classification predictions). The classical component computes the cost or error function (such as classification loss or clustering accuracy) and adjusts the quantum circuit's parameters, iterating until convergence.
  - **Quantum Parameter Optimization**: For clustering and classification tasks, the quantum circuit may have parameters that affect the quantum state preparation (e.g., rotations in the case of angle encoding). The classical optimizer updates these parameters by evaluating the quantum cost function after each quantum circuit execution.
  - **Classical Optimizer Choices**: Common classical optimization algorithms used in this loop include gradient descent, evolutionary algorithms, and Bayesian optimization. These optimizers adjust the parameters of the

quantum circuits to minimize the overall loss function in both clustering and classification problems.

Step 4: Evaluation and Performance Metrics

Once the custom quantum algorithm has been designed and trained, it is crucial to evaluate its performance in comparison to classical algorithms. Key metrics for evaluation include:

- **Clustering Metrics**: For clustering tasks, evaluation metrics include **adjusted Rand index**, **Silhouette score**, and **cluster purity**. These metrics measure how well the algorithm groups similar data points and separates dissimilar ones.
- **Classification Metrics**: For classification tasks, metrics like **accuracy**, **precision**, **recall**, **F1 score**, and **area under the ROC curve (AUC)** are commonly used to assess model performance. The quantum classifier's performance should be benchmarked against classical classifiers like SVM, k-NN, and decision trees.
- **Scalability and Speedup**: Quantum algorithms should be tested for speedup over classical counterparts, particularly in terms of how they scale with increasing dataset size and dimensionality. Quantum algorithms are expected to outperform classical methods for high-dimensional, large-scale problems that involve complex patterns and large feature spaces.

Step 5: Deployment and Real-World Application

After successfully designing, training, and evaluating the quantum machine learning model, the next step is deploying it in a real-world application. This involves integrating the quantum model with classical components for real-time decision-making. Real-world applications of quantum clustering and classification models include:

- **Customer Segmentation**: Quantum clustering can be used to segment customers in e-commerce or finance, enabling companies to target personalized offers and services to specific customer groups.
- **Medical Diagnostics**: Quantum classification algorithms can assist in diagnosing diseases by classifying medical images or patient data, offering potentially faster and more accurate predictions.

- **Recommendation Systems**: Quantum clustering and classification can be used to build advanced recommendation systems by clustering users or products and classifying preferences based on quantum-enhanced data processing.

Designing a custom quantum algorithm for machine learning, such as quantum clustering or classification, provides a powerful and efficient alternative to classical methods. By combining quantum algorithms like quantum k-means and quantum support vector machines with classical optimization techniques, we can solve complex, high-dimensional machine learning tasks that are beyond the reach of traditional algorithms.

With the ongoing advancements in quantum hardware and algorithms, the potential for quantum machine learning to revolutionize industries such as healthcare, finance, and e-commerce is becoming increasingly tangible. By carefully designing quantum circuits and integrating them into hybrid quantum-classical workflows, researchers and practitioners can leverage quantum speedups to tackle some of the most challenging problems in machine learning and data science.

CHAPTER 9: Case Studies: Practical Applications of Quantum ML

DESCRIPTION:

This chapter highlights real-world **case studies** that demonstrate the practical applications of Quantum Machine Learning (QML). Readers will explore how QML is being used across industries, including finance, healthcare, logistics, and chemistry. Through these examples, they will learn to identify problems suitable for quantum solutions, design QML workflows, and evaluate performance in comparison to classical methods.

Case Study 1: Quantum Machine Learning in Financial Forecasting

Introduction: The Role of QML in Finance

The financial industry is an ideal testing ground for quantum machine learning (QML) due to the sector's reliance on predictive analytics, optimization, and pattern recognition in massive datasets. Traditional machine learning models have delivered impressive results in tasks such as portfolio optimization, fraud detection, and stock price prediction. However, the exponential growth in data complexity and the need for enhanced computational efficiency present challenges that classical approaches cannot always overcome. QML, leveraging the quantum properties of superposition, entanglement, and interference, offers the potential to revolutionize financial forecasting by introducing faster, more efficient algorithms for complex tasks.

This case study explores the use of QML models to solve critical financial problems, focusing on portfolio optimization, fraud detection, and stock price prediction. It delves into the design and implementation of hybrid quantum-classical models, highlights key advantages, and discusses the limitations of current technology.

QML in Portfolio Optimization

Problem Definition

Portfolio optimization involves allocating assets to maximize returns while minimizing risks under certain constraints (e.g., budget, regulatory compliance). This task often requires solving quadratic optimization problems, which are computationally expensive for large portfolios using classical methods.

QML Solution: Quantum Approximate Optimization Algorithm (QAOA)

1. **Model Design:**
    - Represent the portfolio optimization problem as a quadratic unconstrained binary optimization (QUBO) problem.
    - Encode the problem into a quantum circuit using QAOA, which leverages a variational quantum algorithm to find approximate solutions to optimization problems.
2. **Implementation:**
    - **Data Encoding:** Encode historical financial data, such as asset returns and covariances, into quantum states using feature maps.

- **Quantum Circuit Construction:** Use Qiskit or TensorFlow Quantum to construct a parameterized quantum circuit for QAOA.
- **Hybrid Optimization:** Combine classical gradient-based optimizers to update the variational parameters of the quantum circuit iteratively.

3. **Results:**
   - Achieved faster convergence to near-optimal solutions compared to classical optimization techniques.
   - Demonstrated the ability to scale QAOA for mid-sized portfolios, reducing computational overhead.

QML in Fraud Detection

Problem Definition

Fraud detection requires identifying anomalous transactions in large datasets, a task characterized by high dimensionality and imbalanced data distribution. Classical machine learning models often struggle with scalability and detecting subtle anomalies.

QML Solution: Quantum Support Vector Machine (QSVM)

1. **Model Design:**
   - Use a QSVM to classify legitimate and fraudulent transactions. QSVMs leverage quantum feature maps to enhance the separability of classes in high-dimensional space.
2. **Implementation:**
   - **Data Preprocessing:** Normalize transactional data and identify features relevant to detecting fraudulent activities.
   - **Quantum Feature Mapping:** Map classical data into a higher-dimensional Hilbert space using quantum kernels.
   - **Model Training:** Train the QSVM using labeled data and evaluate its performance using a validation dataset.
3. **Results:**
   - Enhanced detection of complex fraudulent patterns compared to classical SVMs.
   - Improved performance on highly imbalanced datasets due to quantum-enhanced feature separability.

QML in Stock Price Prediction

Problem Definition

Predicting stock prices involves modeling non-linear dependencies and temporal patterns in financial time series data. Classical methods such as recurrent neural networks (RNNs) and Long Short-Term Memory (LSTM) networks have limitations in capturing long-range dependencies and processing high-dimensional inputs.

QML Solution: Hybrid Quantum-Classical Neural Networks (QNNs)

1. **Model Design:**
    - Integrate parameterized quantum circuits with classical LSTMs to create a hybrid QNN for time-series forecasting.
2. **Implementation:**
    - **Data Encoding:** Encode time-series data (e.g., historical stock prices, trading volumes) into quantum states using amplitude encoding.
    - **Quantum Layer Construction:** Develop a variational quantum circuit with trainable parameters.
    - **Hybrid Training:** Use a classical backpropagation algorithm to optimize both the quantum and classical components of the model.
3. **Results:**
    - Improved accuracy in forecasting volatile stock movements compared to classical LSTM models.
    - Reduced overfitting due to the regularization effect of quantum circuits.

Challenges and Future Opportunities

Challenges:

1. **Hardware Limitations:** Current quantum processors have limited qubits and are prone to noise, which constrains the scalability of QML models.
2. **Data Encoding Complexity:** Encoding large-scale financial datasets into quantum states remains computationally expensive.

3. **Algorithmic Maturity:** Many QML algorithms are still in their experimental phase and lack robust implementations for real-world applications.

Future Opportunities:

1. **Enhanced Hardware:** The advent of fault-tolerant quantum processors will enable larger, more complex QML models.
2. **Improved Algorithms:** Continued research in QML algorithms, particularly for optimization and anomaly detection, will unlock new possibilities for financial applications.
3. **Hybrid Ecosystems:** Advances in hybrid quantum-classical frameworks will facilitate seamless integration of quantum computing into existing financial workflows.

Quantum machine learning offers transformative potential for financial forecasting by addressing challenges associated with computational complexity, data dimensionality, and optimization inefficiencies. Through portfolio optimization, fraud detection, and stock price prediction, QML demonstrates its ability to outperform classical approaches in speed and accuracy. While challenges persist, ongoing advancements in quantum technology and algorithm development signal a promising future for QML in revolutionizing financial analytics.

Case Study 2: Quantum-Enhanced Drug Discovery in Healthcare

Introduction: The Role of Quantum Machine Learning in Healthcare

Drug discovery is a cornerstone of healthcare innovation, involving the identification and development of new therapeutic compounds to combat diseases. Traditional approaches to drug discovery rely heavily on classical computational techniques, which often require years of research and significant financial investment. One of the key bottlenecks in the process is molecular simulation—accurately predicting molecular interactions and chemical properties to identify potential drug candidates.

Quantum machine learning (QML) has the potential to revolutionize this process by leveraging quantum mechanics to simulate molecular structures and dynamics with greater precision. QML techniques, when combined with classical methods, can accelerate drug discovery by enabling faster, more accurate predictions of molecular behavior, reducing the cost and time required for research and development. This case study explores how QML is applied to molecular simulation and drug discovery, focusing on hybrid quantum-classical approaches, practical implementations, and potential real-world impact.

Quantum Applications in Molecular Simulation

Problem Definition

Molecular simulation involves modeling the interactions between atoms and molecules to predict properties such as binding affinities, reaction rates, and toxicity. Classical methods, such as density functional theory (DFT) and molecular dynamics simulations, are computationally intensive and struggle with accurately representing quantum mechanical phenomena in large molecular systems.

Quantum Solution: Variational Quantum Eigensolver (VQE)

1. **Model Design:**
   - Use the VQE algorithm to solve the electronic structure problem of molecules. VQE approximates the ground-state energy of a molecule, which is critical for understanding molecular stability and reactivity.
2. **Implementation:**
   - **Data Encoding:** Encode molecular Hamiltonians into quantum states using second quantization or qubit-mapping techniques.
   - **Quantum Circuit Construction:** Design parameterized quantum circuits to represent molecular wavefunctions.
   - **Hybrid Optimization:** Employ classical optimizers to minimize the energy expectation value of the quantum circuit, iteratively improving the accuracy of the molecular simulation.
3. **Results:**
   - Achieved high-precision simulations for small molecules such as hydrogen and lithium hydride, demonstrating the potential for scaling to more complex systems as quantum hardware improves.

QML in Drug Discovery

Problem Definition

Drug discovery involves identifying potential compounds that can bind to target proteins and modulate their function. Screening large chemical libraries and optimizing lead compounds for efficacy and safety is a resource-intensive process.

Quantum Solution: Quantum Kernel Methods for Drug Screening

1. **Model Design:**
    - Use quantum kernel methods to classify chemical compounds based on their binding affinities to target proteins. Quantum kernels exploit the high-dimensional Hilbert space of quantum systems to enhance the separability of molecular features.
2. **Implementation:**
    - **Feature Extraction:** Generate molecular descriptors using cheminformatics tools.
    - **Quantum Kernel Calculation:** Map molecular features into a quantum Hilbert space and calculate the similarity between compounds using a quantum kernel.
    - **Model Training:** Train a quantum-enhanced support vector machine (QSVM) to classify compounds as "active" or "inactive" based on experimental binding data.
3. **Results:**
    - Improved classification accuracy and reduced false positives compared to classical kernel methods.
    - Enabled faster screening of compound libraries, accelerating the identification of lead candidates.

Hybrid Quantum-Classical Workflows in Drug Discovery

Workflow Overview:

1. **Data Preparation:**
    - Collect experimental and simulated molecular data, including 3D structures, binding affinities, and physicochemical properties.
2. **Quantum Simulation:**
    - Use VQE or other quantum algorithms to model electronic properties of drug candidates.
    - Simulate protein-ligand interactions to predict binding energies and optimize compound structures.
3. **QML Integration:**
    - Combine quantum-generated features with classical machine learning models to predict drug efficacy, toxicity, and pharmacokinetics.

- Use reinforcement learning to iteratively refine compound structures and improve target specificity.

4. **Validation:**
   - Validate QML predictions using laboratory experiments, refining the model based on empirical data.

Real-World Application: Quantum-Accelerated Antiviral Development

During the COVID-19 pandemic, pharmaceutical companies faced immense pressure to identify antiviral compounds rapidly. A QML-based approach could significantly enhance this process:

1. **Target Identification:**
   - Use quantum simulations to model the structure and dynamics of viral proteins, identifying potential binding sites for drug molecules.
2. **Compound Screening:**
   - Apply QML algorithms to screen chemical libraries for molecules with high binding affinities to the target protein.
3. **Optimization:**
   - Use hybrid quantum-classical models to optimize lead compounds for improved efficacy and reduced side effects.
4. **Clinical Translation:**
   - Rapidly transition optimized compounds into preclinical and clinical trials, accelerating the development timeline.

Challenges and Future Opportunities

Challenges:

1. **Hardware Limitations:** Current quantum devices lack the qubit count and error correction needed for large-scale molecular simulations.
2. **Data Encoding:** Encoding complex molecular systems into quantum states is computationally demanding.

3. **Integration Complexity:** Developing seamless workflows between quantum and classical systems remains a significant hurdle.

Future Opportunities:

1. **Fault-Tolerant Quantum Hardware:** Advances in quantum processors will enable more accurate simulations of large molecules.
2. **Improved Algorithms:** Research into more efficient quantum algorithms for molecular simulation and optimization will expand the applicability of QML in drug discovery.
3. **Collaborative Platforms:** Integration of quantum computing into cloud-based platforms like Amazon Braket and IBM Quantum will make QML more accessible to pharmaceutical researchers.

Quantum machine learning offers transformative potential in drug discovery, enabling faster and more accurate molecular simulations, efficient screening of chemical libraries, and optimized drug design. By integrating QML techniques into the pharmaceutical R&D pipeline, researchers can address long-standing challenges in molecular simulation and accelerate the discovery of life-saving therapies. While significant challenges remain, the ongoing evolution of quantum technology promises a future where QML becomes an indispensable tool in healthcare innovation.

Case Study 3: Quantum Optimization for Logistics and Supply Chain

Introduction: The Role of Quantum Optimization in Logistics

In an increasingly interconnected world, the complexity of logistics and supply chain management continues to grow, presenting significant challenges for businesses aiming to optimize their operations. Problems such as route planning, demand forecasting, and resource allocation often involve large-scale optimization tasks that are computationally demanding. These problems are exacerbated by fluctuating demands, supply disruptions, and globalized operations.

Quantum optimization offers a revolutionary approach to addressing these challenges by leveraging quantum algorithms to explore vast solution spaces more efficiently than classical methods. Quantum machine learning (QML) and hybrid quantum-classical algorithms can enable faster, more accurate solutions to logistical optimization problems, improving cost efficiency, delivery times, and overall system reliability.

Quantum Optimization in Logistics

Problem Definition

Logistics optimization involves determining the most efficient way to move goods, allocate resources, and plan delivery routes while minimizing costs and meeting constraints such as delivery deadlines, vehicle capacities, and traffic conditions. Classical algorithms, such as linear programming and heuristic approaches, struggle to scale effectively for large, complex systems.

Quantum Solution: Quantum Approximate Optimization Algorithm (QAOA)

1. **Model Design:**
    - Use the QAOA to solve combinatorial optimization problems such as the Traveling Salesman Problem (TSP), vehicle routing, and network flow optimization.
    - Represent these problems as a graph, where nodes represent delivery locations or resources and edges represent distances or costs.
2. **Implementation:**
    - **Problem Encoding:** Encode the optimization problem into a quantum Hamiltonian, where the ground state corresponds to the optimal solution.
    - **Quantum Circuit Construction:** Design a parameterized quantum circuit to iteratively approximate the ground state of the problem Hamiltonian.
    - **Hybrid Optimization:** Use classical optimizers to adjust the circuit parameters, refining the solution over multiple iterations.
3. **Results:**
    - Demonstrated significant speedups for small to medium-sized problem instances compared to classical solvers, with the potential for scaling as quantum hardware matures.

QML Applications in Supply Chain Management

Problem Definition

Supply chain management requires efficient allocation of resources, inventory optimization, and demand forecasting to ensure smooth operations. These tasks often involve solving high-dimensional, nonlinear optimization problems with uncertain inputs.

Quantum Solution: Quantum Neural Networks (QNNs) for Demand Forecasting

1. **Model Design:**
    - Use QNNs to predict demand patterns based on historical data, enabling better resource allocation and inventory management.
2. **Implementation:**
    - **Data Encoding:** Convert historical sales, seasonal trends, and market conditions into quantum-compatible features.
    - **Quantum Circuit Construction:** Design a QNN with parameterized quantum gates to model complex nonlinear relationships in the data.
    - **Training:** Train the QNN using a hybrid quantum-classical approach, optimizing parameters with classical algorithms while leveraging quantum advantages in feature space exploration.
3. **Results:**
    - Achieved higher prediction accuracy and faster training times compared to classical neural networks for certain datasets.
    - Improved inventory planning and reduced stockouts and overstocking issues.

Hybrid Quantum-Classical Workflows in Logistics and Supply Chain

Workflow Overview:

1. **Data Preparation:**
    - Collect and preprocess data on delivery routes, traffic conditions, warehouse locations, and customer orders.
2. **Quantum Optimization:**
    - Apply QAOA or other quantum algorithms to solve routing and scheduling problems.
    - Use quantum-enhanced reinforcement learning to dynamically adjust routes based on real-time data.
3. **QML Integration:**
    - Combine quantum-generated optimization solutions with classical supply chain management systems to streamline operations.
    - Use QML models to predict demand, allocate resources, and optimize production schedules.

4. **Validation:**
    - Validate quantum-generated solutions using simulation tools and real-world data, iteratively improving model performance.

Real-World Application: Optimizing Last-Mile Delivery

Challenges in Last-Mile Delivery:

- High delivery costs due to inefficient routing and scheduling.
- Variable traffic conditions and unpredictable customer demands.

Quantum Solution:

1. **Route Optimization:**
    - Use QAOA to determine the most efficient routes for delivery vehicles, minimizing travel distance and fuel consumption.
2. **Dynamic Scheduling:**
    - Apply QML models to predict delivery times and adjust schedules dynamically based on real-time traffic and order updates.
3. **Resource Allocation:**
    - Optimize vehicle assignments and load distributions to maximize delivery efficiency.

Results:

- Reduced delivery times and operational costs.
- Improved customer satisfaction through more accurate delivery time estimates.

Benefits of Quantum Optimization in Logistics

1. **Scalability:** Quantum algorithms can handle larger, more complex problem instances as hardware capabilities improve.
2. **Speed:** Faster solution times for optimization problems, enabling real-time decision-making.

3. **Accuracy:** Improved solution quality compared to classical heuristics, reducing inefficiencies.
4. **Cost Savings:** Optimized routes and schedules lead to significant reductions in operational costs.

Challenges and Future Opportunities

Challenges:

1. **Hardware Limitations:** Current quantum processors are limited in qubit count and error rates, restricting problem sizes.
2. **Integration:** Combining quantum solutions with existing supply chain management systems requires robust interfacing and validation.
3. **Data Quality:** High-quality data is essential for accurate modeling and optimization, necessitating effective data collection and preprocessing.

Future Opportunities:

1. **Fault-Tolerant Quantum Computing:** Advances in hardware will enable the scaling of quantum optimization algorithms to larger systems.
2. **Cloud-Based Quantum Platforms:** Services like Amazon Braket and IBM Quantum will democratize access to quantum optimization tools for logistics companies.
3. **Collaborative Solutions:** Partnerships between quantum computing providers and logistics firms will accelerate the development of tailored quantum solutions.

Quantum optimization has the potential to transform logistics and supply chain management by providing faster, more accurate solutions to complex problems. By integrating quantum algorithms with classical systems, businesses can achieve significant improvements in cost efficiency, delivery times, and operational reliability. While challenges remain, the ongoing evolution of quantum technology promises a future where quantum optimization becomes a standard tool for tackling the logistical challenges of a globalized world.

Case Study 4: Quantum Classification in Image and Signal Processing

Introduction: Quantum Machine Learning in Image and Signal Processing

Image and signal processing are critical areas in modern technology, powering applications such as autonomous vehicles, medical imaging, communication systems, and data analysis. These domains require highly efficient and accurate classification techniques to interpret and analyze complex patterns in large datasets. Classical machine learning models, such as convolutional neural networks (CNNs), have achieved remarkable success but are often limited by the computational complexity of large-scale problems.

Quantum machine learning (QML) provides a paradigm shift by introducing the potential for exponential speedups and improved model accuracy in specific tasks. By leveraging quantum states and entanglement, QML enables more efficient data encoding and processing, making it an exciting frontier for image recognition, signal classification, and data filtering.

Quantum Classification: Core Principles

Quantum Data Encoding

- **Amplitude Encoding:** Encodes pixel intensities or signal amplitudes into the quantum state amplitudes. This allows for efficient representation of high-dimensional data in quantum systems.
- **Angle Encoding:** Maps data points into quantum states through rotation gates, preserving critical features while reducing redundancy.
- **Hybrid Encoding:** Combines classical preprocessing with quantum encoding to handle noise and improve model robustness.

Quantum Feature Space Exploration

Quantum systems excel at exploring high-dimensional feature spaces. By representing data in a quantum Hilbert space, QML algorithms can uncover patterns and relationships that might be computationally prohibitive for classical systems.

Entanglement and Superposition for Classification

Quantum superposition enables simultaneous evaluation of multiple possibilities, while entanglement allows for capturing correlations between data features. These properties enhance the discriminative power of QML classifiers.

Application in Image Recognition

Problem Definition

Image recognition involves classifying visual data into categories based on patterns in pixel intensities, shapes, and textures. Tasks include object detection, facial recognition, and anomaly detection in industrial applications.

Quantum Neural Networks (QNNs) for Image Recognition

1. **Model Design:**
   - Use parameterized quantum circuits (PQCs) as the core building blocks of QNNs.
   - Combine PQCs with classical preprocessing layers to handle noise and reduce dimensionality.
2. **Implementation:**
   - **Data Encoding:** Map image data into quantum states using amplitude or angle encoding.
   - **Quantum Circuit Construction:** Construct a quantum circuit with multiple layers of parameterized gates to learn image features.
   - **Training:** Train the QNN using hybrid quantum-classical optimization algorithms, such as gradient descent, to minimize classification error.
3. **Results:**
   - Achieved high accuracy on benchmark image datasets (e.g., MNIST) with fewer computational resources compared to classical models.
   - Demonstrated robustness to noise and variability in input data.

Case Example: Quantum-Enhanced Medical Imaging

QNNs were used to classify MRI scans into categories such as "healthy" and "diseased." The quantum approach improved classification accuracy and reduced processing time, aiding early disease detection.

Application in Signal Classification

Problem Definition

Signal classification involves analyzing time-series data, such as audio signals, electromagnetic waves, or communication signals, to identify patterns and categorize inputs. Applications range from speech recognition to radar signal analysis.

Variational Quantum Classifiers (VQCs) for Signal Processing

1. **Model Design:**
    - Use variational quantum classifiers that adaptively learn signal features through quantum circuits.
    - Incorporate temporal and frequency domain analysis for signal representation.
2. **Implementation:**
    - **Data Encoding:** Encode signal data as quantum states using Fourier transform techniques.
    - **Quantum Circuit Construction:** Design PQCs to model signal features, using entanglement to capture dependencies across time and frequency.
    - **Training:** Optimize circuit parameters with classical solvers to minimize misclassification rates.
3. **Results:**
    - Improved classification accuracy for complex signals, such as identifying spoken words or detecting anomalies in radar signals.
    - Reduced computational overhead compared to deep classical models.

Case Example: Quantum-Based Audio Classification

VQCs were employed to classify audio signals into categories such as "speech," "music," and "noise." The quantum model demonstrated faster training times and higher accuracy, particularly for noisy datasets.

Data Filtering and Noise Reduction

Problem Definition

Filtering and noise reduction are essential preprocessing steps in both image and signal processing. Traditional methods rely on algorithms like wavelet transforms or convolutional filters, which can be computationally intensive for high-dimensional data.

Quantum Filters:

1. **Model Design:**
    - Quantum filters use quantum circuits to perform operations equivalent to convolution or Fourier transforms, enabling efficient noise reduction.
2. **Implementation:**
    - **Quantum Noise Filtering:** Apply quantum gates to remove noise components while preserving critical features.
    - **Hybrid Filtering:** Combine quantum filtering with classical postprocessing for enhanced results.
3. **Results:**
    - Improved signal-to-noise ratio in processed data.
    - Faster execution times for high-dimensional datasets.

Hybrid Quantum-Classical Workflows for Classification

Workflow Overview:

1. **Data Preparation:**
    - Preprocess raw data (e.g., resizing images, normalizing signals) and encode it into quantum-compatible formats.
2. **Quantum Model Training:**
    - Train QNNs or VQCs using a hybrid quantum-classical optimization loop.
3. **Integration:**
    - Integrate quantum models with classical systems for deployment in real-world applications, such as autonomous vehicles or communication networks.
4. **Evaluation:**

- Validate model performance using metrics like accuracy, precision, recall, and F1-score.

Challenges and Future Directions

Challenges:

1. **Hardware Constraints:** Current quantum devices are limited in qubit count and coherence time, affecting scalability.
2. **Noise Sensitivity:** Quantum systems are inherently sensitive to noise, requiring robust error mitigation techniques.
3. **Data Encoding Overhead:** Efficiently encoding high-dimensional data into quantum states remains a technical challenge.

Future Opportunities:

1. **Fault-Tolerant Quantum Hardware:** Advances in hardware will enable larger and more reliable quantum systems.
2. **Quantum-Classical Co-Design:** Improved integration of quantum models with classical systems will enhance applicability.
3. **Industry-Specific Solutions:** Tailored quantum classification models for specific domains, such as healthcare or telecommunications, will drive adoption.

Quantum machine learning is poised to revolutionize image and signal processing by providing more efficient and accurate classification models. By leveraging quantum properties such as superposition and entanglement, QML algorithms enable faster, more scalable solutions to complex tasks. While challenges remain, the rapid evolution of quantum technology and hybrid workflows promises a future where quantum classification becomes a cornerstone of next-generation image and signal processing applications.

Evaluating QML Solutions: Performance and Scalability

Introduction

Quantum Machine Learning (QML) introduces a groundbreaking approach to solving complex problems in data analysis, optimization, and artificial intelligence. While QML holds the promise of quantum speed-ups and unique computational advantages, it is critical to rigorously evaluate its performance and scalability in real-world applications. This chapter provides a comprehensive framework for analyzing QML solutions, comparing them with classical machine learning (ML) models, and addressing their practical limitations and future potential.

Key Performance Metrics for QML Models

To evaluate QML solutions effectively, several performance metrics are considered:

1. Accuracy and Precision

- **Definition:** The proportion of correct predictions made by the model, evaluated using metrics like accuracy, precision, recall, and F1-score.
- **QML Advantage:** For certain problems, QML models can achieve higher accuracy by leveraging quantum-enhanced feature spaces.
- **Example:** A Quantum Neural Network (QNN) used for image classification may outperform a classical Convolutional Neural Network (CNN) on specific datasets.

2. Computational Efficiency

- **Definition:** The time and resources required to train and execute the model.
- **QML Advantage:** Quantum algorithms like the Quantum Approximate Optimization Algorithm (QAOA) can solve optimization problems more efficiently than classical algorithms under specific conditions.
- **Limitations:** Current quantum hardware has significant overhead in terms of noise mitigation and limited qubit count.

3. Resource Utilization

- **Definition:** The effective use of hardware resources, such as qubits, quantum gates, and classical computational support.
- **Trade-off:** While QML can reduce computational complexity for specific tasks, encoding data into quantum states and hybrid integration can introduce overhead.

4. Robustness to Noise

- **Definition:** The ability of the model to maintain accuracy and stability in noisy environments, a critical factor for real-world applications.
- **Challenges:** QML models are inherently sensitive to quantum decoherence and gate errors, requiring sophisticated error mitigation strategies.

Comparing QML and Classical ML Models

1. Computational Complexity

- **Classical ML:** Algorithms like Gradient Boosting or Support Vector Machines (SVMs) can handle large datasets efficiently but may struggle with high-dimensional feature spaces.
- **QML:** Algorithms like Quantum Support Vector Machines (QSVMs) or Variational Quantum Classifiers (VQCs) excel in high-dimensional spaces by leveraging quantum parallelism.

2. Data Requirements

- **Classical ML:** Relies on large, labeled datasets for training.
- **QML:** Can work with smaller datasets due to quantum-enhanced sampling but may require preprocessing for quantum state encoding.

3. Applicability to Tasks

- **Classical ML:** Broadly applicable to most current problems, supported by mature tools and frameworks.
- **QML:** Currently most advantageous in niche applications, such as optimization, quantum chemistry, and specific machine learning tasks like clustering or dimensionality reduction.

Scalability of QML Solutions

1. Hardware Scalability

- **Challenges:**
    - Limited qubit count in current quantum devices.

- High error rates and decoherence in quantum systems.
- Bottlenecks in quantum-classical communication.

- **Future Opportunities:**
  - Advancements in fault-tolerant quantum computing.
  - Scalable quantum error correction techniques.

2. Algorithmic Scalability

- **QML Algorithms:** Many QML algorithms demonstrate theoretical scalability advantages for large datasets.
- **Example:** The Quantum Fourier Transform (QFT) scales logarithmically compared to its classical counterpart, enabling efficient processing of high-dimensional data.

3. Hybrid Workflows

- **Integration:** Scalability improves with hybrid quantum-classical workflows, where quantum systems handle computationally intensive tasks while classical systems manage data preprocessing and model evaluation.
- **Example:** Variational Quantum Eigensolvers (VQEs) combined with classical optimizers for scalable problem-solving in quantum chemistry and optimization.

Case Studies: Performance and Scalability Analysis

Case Study 1: Portfolio Optimization in Finance

- **Setup:** Quantum Approximate Optimization Algorithm (QAOA) versus classical Genetic Algorithm (GA) for portfolio allocation.
- **Findings:**
  - QAOA demonstrated faster convergence for smaller problem sizes but faced hardware limitations for larger datasets.
  - Classical GA remained more practical for large-scale problems due to mature software and infrastructure.

Case Study 2: Quantum-enhanced Image Classification

- **Setup:** Quantum Neural Network (QNN) versus Convolutional Neural Network (CNN) for handwritten digit recognition.
- **Findings:**
    - QNN achieved higher accuracy on small datasets, leveraging quantum-enhanced feature mapping.
    - CNN outperformed QNN in large-scale scenarios due to noise and resource constraints in quantum hardware.

Challenges in Evaluating QML Solutions

1. Limited Benchmarks

- Lack of standardized benchmarks for comparing QML and classical ML models across different problem domains.

2. Data Encoding Overhead

- Significant computational cost associated with encoding classical data into quantum states.

3. Noise and Error Rates

- High sensitivity to noise limits the reliability of current QML solutions.

4. Hardware Constraints

- Scalability is restricted by the limited capabilities of existing quantum processors.

Future Directions for Performance and Scalability

1. Improved Hardware

- Development of error-tolerant quantum processors with higher qubit counts.

2. Advanced Algorithms

- Research into more robust and scalable QML algorithms, such as error-resilient Variational Quantum Algorithms (VQAs).

3. Standardized Evaluation Frameworks

- Establishing benchmarks and metrics to compare QML and classical ML solutions comprehensively.

4. Industry-Specific Applications

- Developing tailored QML models for specific industries, such as healthcare, finance, and logistics.

Evaluating the performance and scalability of Quantum Machine Learning solutions is essential for understanding their practical advantages and limitations. While QML shows great promise in terms of computational efficiency and unique capabilities, its current applications are constrained by hardware and algorithmic challenges. By addressing these limitations and integrating QML with classical systems, we can unlock its full potential for solving real-world problems at scale. The future of QML will depend on advancements in quantum technology, innovative algorithms, and rigorous evaluation methodologies to establish it as a transformative force in machine learning.

CHAPTER 10: Comparing Classical vs. Quantum Approaches

DESCRIPTION:

This chapter explores a detailed **comparison between classical and quantum machine learning approaches**, focusing on their performance, scalability, and efficiency. Readers will analyze key differences, advantages, and limitations of both paradigms through real-world examples and benchmarks. By the end of this chapter, readers will have a clear understanding of where quantum machine learning provides a meaningful edge and when classical methods remain sufficient.

Fundamental Differences Between Classical and Quantum Machine Learning

Machine learning, at its core, leverages mathematical models to identify patterns and make predictions from data. Classical machine learning operates within the well-defined boundaries of classical computation, utilizing digital hardware and algorithms rooted in deterministic logic. Quantum machine learning (QML), on the other hand, integrates principles of quantum mechanics, introducing new paradigms that challenge the conventions of classical models. This section explores the fundamental differences between the two approaches, providing a comprehensive understanding of their unique characteristics, strengths, and limitations.

---

1. Data Representation

Classical Machine Learning:

- In classical ML, data is represented as vectors in high-dimensional feature spaces, often requiring transformations or embeddings to fit the model's requirements. For instance, a digital image is represented as a grid of pixel intensity values.
- Classical models rely on deterministic algorithms to manipulate these data representations, limiting their ability to explore exponentially large solution spaces.

Quantum Machine Learning:

- QML leverages quantum states to represent data. In a quantum system, data is encoded in qubits, which can exist in a superposition of states (0 and 1 simultaneously). This allows quantum systems to represent complex, high-dimensional data in fewer resources compared to classical systems.
- Techniques like amplitude encoding and quantum feature maps enable QML models to embed classical data into a quantum state, enhancing the expressive power of the system.

Key Advantage: The ability to represent data in exponentially large Hilbert spaces makes QML particularly suited for tasks that involve highly entangled or complex datasets.

---

2. Computational Speed and Parallelism

Classical Machine Learning:

- Classical ML models process data sequentially or in parallel across multiple processors, limited by the number of physical computational units.
- Algorithms like gradient descent and support vector machines (SVMs) require iterative optimization, which can become computationally expensive for high-dimensional datasets.

Quantum Machine Learning:

- Quantum systems exploit quantum parallelism, allowing computations to occur simultaneously across multiple states. For example, a quantum circuit can evaluate numerous possible solutions in a single step, drastically reducing computation time.
- Algorithms like the Variational Quantum Eigensolver (VQE) and Quantum Approximate Optimization Algorithm (QAOA) are designed to take advantage of this parallelism, providing potential speed-ups for optimization and learning tasks.

Key Advantage: QML promises exponential or polynomial speed-ups for specific tasks, such as large-scale matrix manipulations and combinatorial optimization, compared to their classical counterparts.

---

3. Algorithm Design

Classical Machine Learning:

- Classical ML relies on established algorithms such as neural networks, decision trees, and k-means clustering. These algorithms are designed with deterministic logic, optimized for traditional hardware.
- Many classical ML techniques struggle with computational scalability as datasets grow in size or complexity.

Quantum Machine Learning:

- QML algorithms, such as Quantum Support Vector Machines (QSVM) and Quantum Principal Component Analysis (qPCA), are fundamentally different in their design, leveraging quantum phenomena like entanglement, superposition, and interference.
- QML introduces hybrid algorithms, which combine quantum circuits with classical optimization techniques. For instance, parameterized quantum circuits (PQC) are trained using classical gradient-based methods, creating a synergy between classical and quantum systems.

Key Advantage: Quantum algorithms can explore solution spaces in novel ways, potentially identifying patterns or solutions unattainable by classical models.

---

4. Scalability and Resource Utilization

Classical Machine Learning:

- Classical ML models scale linearly with the number of processors or computational units, often requiring large data centers to handle massive datasets.
- Resource constraints, such as memory and processing power, limit the scalability of classical approaches.

Quantum Machine Learning:

- Quantum systems offer the potential to scale non-linearly by representing and processing data in higher-dimensional spaces with fewer physical qubits.
- However, quantum hardware is still in its infancy, with current systems (NISQ devices) limited in qubit count and prone to noise. Scalability remains a theoretical advantage that depends on future advancements in quantum hardware.

Key Challenge: While QML holds promise for scalability, practical implementation is hindered by hardware limitations and error rates.

---

5. Interpretability and Ecosystem Maturity

Classical Machine Learning:

- Classical ML benefits from decades of research, mature frameworks (e.g., TensorFlow, PyTorch), and well-documented algorithms.
- Models like decision trees and linear regression are highly interpretable, while deep learning models require additional techniques (e.g., SHAP values) for explanation.

Quantum Machine Learning:

- QML is an emerging field with rapidly evolving tools and frameworks like TensorFlow Quantum, Qiskit, and PennyLane.
- Quantum algorithms are inherently less interpretable due to the probabilistic nature of quantum mechanics. Understanding quantum states and operations requires advanced knowledge, making QML less accessible to the broader ML community.

Key Insight: While classical ML enjoys a robust ecosystem, QML is still developing, with many tools and methodologies in experimental stages.

---

6. Real-World Applications

Classical Machine Learning:

- Classical ML excels in practical applications like image recognition, natural language processing, and autonomous systems.
- Its reliability and established infrastructure make it the default choice for most industries.

Quantum Machine Learning:

- QML shows promise in niche areas such as molecular simulation, optimization in logistics, and cryptographic analysis, where quantum phenomena provide a significant edge.
- Hybrid quantum-classical models are being explored to combine the strengths of both paradigms, particularly in tasks involving large-scale optimization and high-dimensional feature spaces.

Key Perspective: QML is not a replacement for classical ML but a complementary tool designed to solve specific classes of problems more efficiently.

Classical and quantum machine learning represent two distinct computational paradigms with unique strengths and limitations. While classical ML continues to dominate real-world applications due to its maturity and reliability, QML holds transformative potential for solving problems that are computationally infeasible for classical systems. By understanding the fundamental differences in data representation, computational speed, algorithm design, and scalability, practitioners can identify scenarios where QML offers a tangible advantage. As quantum hardware evolves, the integration of classical and quantum models will likely define the future of machine learning, enabling breakthroughs across diverse fields.

Performance Benchmarks: Classical vs. Quantum Algorithms

The rapidly evolving field of quantum computing has introduced the potential for quantum algorithms to outperform their classical counterparts in specific machine learning tasks. Understanding how quantum machine learning (QML) algorithms compare to traditional classical methods in terms of performance is essential for identifying their practical value and applicability. This section provides an in-depth exploration of performance benchmarks, focusing on speed, accuracy, scalability, and computational efficiency, while analyzing key classical algorithms such as linear regression and clustering against quantum algorithms like Quantum Principal Component Analysis (qPCA) and Quantum Fourier Transform (QFT)-based models.

---

1. Speed and Computational Efficiency

Classical Algorithms:

- Classical algorithms process data sequentially or through parallel computing systems, with efficiency depending on hardware and algorithmic optimizations.
- Linear regression and clustering (e.g., k-means) rely on iterative optimization processes that scale linearly or polynomially with the size of the data and number of features. For example:
    - Linear regression involves solving systems of linear equations, which scales as $O(n^3)$ for matrix inversion, where n is the number of features.
    - Clustering requires calculating distances between data points, which scales as $O(k \cdot n \cdot d)$, where k is the number of clusters, n is the number of data points, and d is the dimensionality of the data.

Quantum Algorithms:

- Quantum models leverage quantum parallelism and phenomena like superposition to process multiple possibilities simultaneously.
- For instance, qPCA can approximate principal components exponentially faster than classical PCA under certain conditions, scaling as $O(\log(n))$ compared to classical PCA's $O(n^2)$.
- QFT-based models achieve significant speed-ups in operations such as data transformation and encoding. The QFT operates in $O(n^2)$ compared to the classical Fast Fourier Transform (FFT), which scales as $O(n \log(n))$, with further improvements depending on circuit optimizations.

Key Benchmark:
Quantum algorithms, particularly qPCA, demonstrate exponential or polynomial speed-ups over classical methods in tasks where data structure or problem complexity benefits from quantum parallelism.

---

2. Accuracy and Error Rates

Classical Algorithms:

- Classical algorithms produce deterministic outputs, and their accuracy depends on factors like model design, hyperparameter tuning, and the quality of input data.
- Techniques like regularization and cross-validation help mitigate overfitting and ensure generalizability, but these approaches can become computationally intensive for large datasets.

Quantum Algorithms:

- Quantum algorithms are inherently probabilistic, with outcomes depending on the measurement of quantum states. This introduces variability in accuracy and necessitates multiple runs to achieve reliable results.
- In tasks like quantum-enhanced clustering or classification, QML models have shown comparable or superior accuracy to classical models when applied to synthetic or quantum-native datasets.

- However, noise and decoherence in current quantum devices (NISQ systems) can degrade performance, requiring error mitigation techniques.

Key Benchmark:
Accuracy comparisons depend on the application and dataset. Quantum algorithms often excel in high-dimensional or highly entangled data spaces but may struggle with noise on real hardware.

---

3. Scalability and Resource Utilization

Classical Algorithms:

- Classical models scale with available computational resources, often requiring substantial memory and processing power for large datasets.
- For example, classical clustering algorithms like k-means become impractical for datasets with millions of features or clusters without distributed computing.

Quantum Algorithms:

- Quantum algorithms encode data into qubits, offering exponential data representation capabilities. This allows QML models to handle problems with high-dimensional feature spaces more efficiently.
- Resource limitations in current quantum hardware (e.g., limited qubit count, connectivity) pose challenges to scalability, but hybrid quantum-classical systems mitigate this by offloading resource-intensive tasks to classical processors.

Key Benchmark:
Quantum models have the theoretical advantage in scalability for specific tasks, but practical implementation depends on advancements in hardware.

---

4. Comparative Analysis of Specific Algorithms

a. Linear Regression vs. Quantum Linear Solver (HHL Algorithm)

- The Harrow-Hassidim-Lloyd (HHL) algorithm is a quantum method for solving linear systems of equations, providing exponential speed-ups under certain conditions.
- Classical linear regression requires $O(n^3)$ operations for matrix inversion, while HHL scales logarithmically with the size of the matrix, $O(\log(n))$, assuming a well-conditioned matrix and efficient quantum subroutines.

b. Classical PCA vs. Quantum PCA (qPCA)

- Classical PCA computes eigenvectors of the covariance matrix, scaling as $O(n^2 \cdot m)$, where n is the number of data points and mmm is the dimensionality of features.
- qPCA leverages quantum state preparation to approximate eigenvectors exponentially faster, $O(\log(n))$, given suitable quantum resources.
- Applications: Dimensionality reduction for high-dimensional datasets, such as image compression and feature extraction.

c. Clustering (k-means) vs. Quantum k-means

- Classical k-means requires iterative distance calculations and reassignments, scaling as $O(k \cdot n \cdot d)$.
- Quantum k-means employs quantum distance estimation and amplitude amplification to reduce computational overhead, scaling as $O(\sqrt{n})$ in certain cases.
- Applications: Customer segmentation, genetic data analysis, and image segmentation.

d. FFT vs. QFT

- Classical FFT scales as $O(n \log(n))$ for transforming time-series data, while QFT achieves $O(n^2)$ or faster with optimized circuits.
- QFT-based models are particularly advantageous for applications involving periodic patterns, such as signal processing and speech recognition.

---

5. Limitations and Practical Considerations

- **Classical Algorithms:** Classical models are reliable and robust for well-structured datasets but face limitations in computational scalability and efficiency for complex, high-dimensional problems.

- **Quantum Algorithms:** Quantum methods offer theoretical speed-ups but face hardware constraints, noise, and challenges in integrating with classical systems. Hybrid approaches are crucial for practical applications.

Performance benchmarks reveal that quantum algorithms hold transformative potential for tasks involving high-dimensional data, optimization, and feature extraction. While classical methods remain dominant in real-world applications due to their maturity and reliability, QML is poised to redefine computational paradigms for specific use cases. By analyzing key metrics like speed, accuracy, and scalability, researchers and practitioners can better understand the trade-offs and opportunities of adopting quantum approaches. As quantum hardware evolves, the balance between classical and quantum methodologies will increasingly favor hybrid solutions, unlocking unprecedented capabilities across industries.

Resource Requirements and Scalability: Assessing Quantum ML Models vs. Classical Approaches

The deployment of machine learning (ML) models, whether classical or quantum, requires a clear understanding of the computational resources they demand and their scalability potential. Quantum Machine Learning (QML) introduces unique paradigms that leverage quantum mechanics to process data in ways classical models cannot, especially for high-dimensional or complex datasets. However, these advantages come with distinct resource requirements and scalability challenges. In this section, we will examine the computational resources—such as memory, processors, and hardware infrastructure—required for QML models compared to classical ML, and evaluate the scalability of both approaches in real-world applications.

---

1. Memory Requirements

Classical ML Models:

- Classical ML models represent data as binary values and rely on memory to store data matrices, model parameters, and intermediate calculations.
- Memory usage scales linearly or quadratically with the size of the dataset and the dimensionality of the features. For example:
    - A dataset with n samples and d features requires $O(n \cdot d)$ memory for storage.

  - Algorithms like PCA or clustering may additionally require $O(d^2)$ memory for covariance matrices or distance calculations.

Quantum ML Models:

- QML models encode data into quantum states using qubits, which offer exponential data representation compared to classical memory. For example:
  - n qubits can represent 2^n states simultaneously, enabling efficient encoding of high-dimensional data.
  - However, the quantum memory advantage is theoretical and heavily dependent on efficient quantum state preparation, which can require significant classical preprocessing.
- Current quantum hardware (NISQ devices) is limited in terms of qubit coherence and connectivity, often constraining the size of the datasets that can be effectively processed.

Key Insight:
While quantum memory can theoretically handle exponentially large datasets, practical implementations are constrained by hardware limitations and the overhead of data encoding.

---

2. Processor and Hardware Requirements

Classical ML Models:

- Classical models rely on CPUs, GPUs, or TPUs to perform calculations. The choice of processor depends on the task:
  - **CPUs** are optimal for sequential tasks and smaller datasets.
  - **GPUs/TPUs** excel at parallelized tasks like deep learning and matrix operations, significantly reducing computation times for large datasets.
- Classical hardware scalability is well-established, with distributed computing frameworks (e.g., Hadoop, Spark) enabling horizontal scaling across multiple nodes.

Quantum ML Models:

- Quantum models depend on quantum processors, which use qubits to execute computations. Quantum hardware requirements include:

- **Qubit Count:** The number of qubits determines the size and complexity of the problem that can be addressed. Current devices typically range from 50–100 qubits, far below the requirements for large-scale problems.
- **Error Rates:** Quantum gates must operate with minimal noise to ensure reliable results. Error correction significantly increases resource requirements.
- **Hybrid Systems:** Many QML implementations rely on hybrid quantum-classical systems, where classical processors handle data preprocessing, result interpretation, and error mitigation.

Key Insight:
Quantum processors are in their infancy, with resource constraints significantly impacting their scalability. Hybrid systems are critical for practical applications in the near term.

---

3. Scalability: Algorithmic and Hardware Considerations

Classical ML Models:

- **Algorithmic Scalability:** Classical models scale predictably with the size of the dataset and the complexity of the task. For example:
  - Gradient descent optimization scales linearly with the number of parameters.
  - Distributed frameworks (e.g., MapReduce, MPI) ensure scalability by dividing data across multiple nodes.
- **Hardware Scalability:** Adding more CPUs, GPUs, or TPUs to a cluster enables near-linear scaling for many tasks, though communication overhead can become a bottleneck.

Quantum ML Models:

- **Algorithmic Scalability:** Quantum algorithms, such as Quantum Principal Component Analysis (qPCA) and Grover's search, offer polynomial or exponential speed-ups for specific tasks. However:
  - These speed-ups depend on the problem's structure (e.g., sparsity, symmetry).
  - Scaling beyond a certain dataset size may require more qubits than current hardware can provide.
- **Hardware Scalability:** Scaling quantum systems involves increasing qubit count, improving qubit fidelity, and enhancing connectivity. Challenges include:

- Decoherence: The quantum states of qubits degrade over time, limiting computation length.
- Quantum error correction: Correcting errors requires redundant qubits, often increasing qubit requirements by an order of magnitude.

Key Insight:
Quantum algorithms exhibit superior algorithmic scalability for problems that align with quantum speed-up criteria, but hardware scalability remains a significant bottleneck.

---

4. Power Consumption

Classical ML Models:

- Modern GPUs and TPUs consume significant power but have been optimized for efficiency through advancements in chip design and cooling systems.
- Data centers hosting classical ML models require extensive energy resources, but renewable energy adoption mitigates environmental impact.

Quantum ML Models:

- Quantum processors operate at near-zero temperatures to maintain qubit coherence, necessitating advanced cooling systems such as dilution refrigerators.
- While quantum computations themselves consume minimal power, the infrastructure for maintaining a quantum computer significantly increases energy costs.

Key Insight:
Quantum computing infrastructure demands higher power per device compared to classical systems, though this is offset by the reduced computational complexity for specific tasks.

---

5. Cost Analysis

Classical ML Models:

- Hardware costs for classical systems scale predictably with performance requirements. Cloud platforms (e.g., AWS, Google Cloud) offer scalable solutions for classical ML models, reducing upfront costs.
- Costs are proportional to computation time, storage requirements, and network bandwidth.

Quantum ML Models:

- Quantum systems remain prohibitively expensive, with costs tied to both hardware development and maintenance.
- Access to quantum computers is typically available through cloud platforms (e.g., IBM Quantum, D-Wave, Rigetti), where users pay per quantum circuit execution.

Key Insight:
Quantum ML is currently more expensive than classical ML, but costs are expected to decrease as quantum hardware matures and scales.

---

6. Real-World Examples of Resource Utilization

Classical ML Applications:

- Training a deep learning model (e.g., ResNet) on a large dataset using GPUs in a distributed environment. Resource requirements include terabytes of memory and thousands of processing cores.
- Running clustering algorithms on massive customer datasets using Spark for distributed processing.

Quantum ML Applications:

- Performing qPCA on a small but high-dimensional dataset using IBM's quantum cloud platform, requiring high-quality qubits and noise mitigation techniques.
- Solving an optimization problem (e.g., portfolio optimization) with Quantum Approximate Optimization Algorithm (QAOA), leveraging hybrid quantum-classical systems for parameter tuning.

Quantum Machine Learning models offer revolutionary potential in resource efficiency for high-dimensional and complex datasets, with the ability to leverage quantum phenomena like superposition and entanglement. However, the practical implementation of QML is constrained by the current state of quantum hardware, which imposes significant resource limitations and scalability challenges. Classical ML models, in contrast, benefit from mature, scalable hardware and algorithms optimized for modern computational infrastructures. While QML holds the promise of exponential improvements in specific domains, hybrid quantum-classical approaches are the most practical solution for addressing real-world problems today. As quantum hardware advances, we can expect a gradual shift towards broader adoption of QML models in scalable applications.

When to Use Quantum Over Classical Approaches: A Decision-Making Framework

Quantum Machine Learning (QML) offers promising advantages for solving specific classes of problems, particularly those involving high-dimensional data, complex optimization challenges, or computational tasks that scale poorly with classical approaches. However, quantum technologies are still in their infancy, and their application must be carefully evaluated based on the problem's requirements, available resources, and the readiness of quantum hardware. This section outlines a comprehensive decision-making framework to help determine when QML solutions are preferable over classical methods, offering explicit considerations for problem size, complexity, resource constraints, and scalability.

---

1. Key Factors in Choosing Quantum Over Classical Approaches

To decide whether quantum approaches are appropriate, evaluate the following factors:

1.1 Problem Size and Structure

Quantum algorithms excel in processing high-dimensional or structured data efficiently:

- **When to Use Quantum Approaches:**
  - The problem involves data or computation that scales exponentially with input size, such as molecular simulations, large-scale optimization, or feature-rich datasets.
  - The data exhibits specific structures (e.g., sparsity or periodicity) that align with quantum speed-ups, such as in Quantum Principal Component Analysis (qPCA).
- **When to Use Classical Approaches:**

- The problem scales polynomially or linearly, making classical methods computationally efficient (e.g., small regression tasks or low-dimensional clustering).
- No quantum advantage has been theoretically proven or practically demonstrated for the problem type.

1.2 Computational Complexity

Quantum approaches are suited for problems where classical methods face exponential slowdowns:

- **When to Use Quantum Approaches:**
  - Solving combinatorial optimization problems with a large search space (e.g., the Traveling Salesman Problem) using algorithms like Quantum Approximate Optimization Algorithm (QAOA).
  - Machine learning tasks involving data encodings that map naturally to quantum states, enabling faster convergence.
- **When to Use Classical Approaches:**
  - The problem complexity is low, and classical heuristic or approximate methods provide near-optimal solutions efficiently.

1.3 Quantum Speed-Up Potential

Quantum speed-ups are achievable only for problems with quantum-advantaged algorithms:

- **When to Use Quantum Approaches:**
  - The problem involves tasks like factoring, search, or matrix manipulation where algorithms like Shor's or Grover's can deliver exponential or quadratic speed-ups.
  - There is empirical evidence of quantum speed-up over classical algorithms, even on noisy intermediate-scale quantum (NISQ) devices.
- **When to Use Classical Approaches:**
  - Quantum speed-up cannot be realized due to lack of suitable quantum algorithms or limitations of current quantum hardware.

---

2. Resource Availability

2.1 Quantum Hardware and Software Readiness

The practical feasibility of quantum computing is limited by hardware constraints:

- **When to Use Quantum Approaches:**
    - Access to high-quality quantum hardware (e.g., IBM Quantum, Rigetti) with sufficient qubit fidelity and coherence time is available.
    - The problem can be executed on a hybrid quantum-classical architecture, compensating for quantum hardware limitations.
- **When to Use Classical Approaches:**
    - Quantum hardware resources are unavailable or insufficient for the problem scale.
    - Classical hardware (e.g., GPUs, TPUs) provides a faster and more reliable alternative for the problem.

2.2 Budgetary and Operational Constraints

Quantum computing currently incurs higher costs and resource demands:

- **When to Use Quantum Approaches:**
    - The potential benefits (e.g., accuracy, speed-up) outweigh the costs of quantum computation, especially in high-stakes applications like drug discovery or financial forecasting.
- **When to Use Classical Approaches:**
    - Budgetary constraints make classical cloud platforms a more economical choice for computation.

---

3. Scalability and Long-Term Considerations

3.1 Problem Growth Over Time

Quantum computing is future-ready for problems expected to grow in scale:

- **When to Use Quantum Approaches:**

    - The problem is expected to grow exponentially in data size or complexity, necessitating scalable solutions like quantum-enhanced clustering or feature reduction.
- **When to Use Classical Approaches:**
    - The problem's scale will remain manageable with classical methods due to slow growth or low dimensionality.

3.2 Algorithm Maturity and Industry Use Cases

The maturity of quantum algorithms and real-world validation influences their applicability:

- **When to Use Quantum Approaches:**
    - Proven quantum algorithms exist for the problem domain (e.g., VQE for molecular simulation, QAOA for optimization).
    - Industry use cases have demonstrated practical quantum advantages for similar problems.
- **When to Use Classical Approaches:**
    - Quantum algorithms are still experimental, with no clear empirical evidence of superiority for the specific task.

---

4. Hybrid Quantum-Classical Solutions

In many cases, the optimal approach may combine quantum and classical computing:

- **When to Use Hybrid Approaches:**
    - Quantum components address specific computational bottlenecks (e.g., feature selection or optimization), while classical components handle data preprocessing and result interpretation.
    - The hybrid model leverages the strengths of both paradigms, providing practical solutions even with current NISQ limitations.
- **Examples of Hybrid Use Cases:**
    - Using quantum annealing for supply chain optimization while employing classical solvers for demand forecasting.

- Employing quantum kernels for feature mapping in support vector machines, with classical training of the SVM.

---

5. Real-World Scenarios for Decision-Making

Scenario 1: Financial Forecasting

- **Use Quantum:** Portfolio optimization with numerous assets and complex constraints (QAOA).
- **Use Classical:** Simple time-series predictions for stock prices using ARIMA or LSTMs.

Scenario 2: Healthcare and Drug Discovery

- **Use Quantum:** Molecular simulation requiring accurate modeling of electron configurations (VQE).
- **Use Classical:** Analyzing patient records for disease prediction using classical supervised learning.

Scenario 3: Image Recognition

- **Use Quantum:** Signal processing tasks with high-dimensional feature spaces, leveraging quantum Fourier transforms.
- **Use Classical:** Small-scale image classification tasks using convolutional neural networks (CNNs).

---

6. Decision-Making Framework

Criterion	Quantum Approach	Classical Approach
Problem Size	High-dimensional, complex datasets	Low-dimensional, straightforward datasets
Computational Complexity	Exponential or quadratic growth in runtime	Polynomial or linear runtime

Speed-Up Potential	Quantum algorithms with proven speed-ups	No quantum advantage demonstrated
Hardware Availability	Access to reliable quantum systems	Limited or no quantum hardware access
Budget	High-stakes problems justifying quantum costs	Budget-sensitive applications
Scalability	Problems expected to grow exponentially	Problems expected to remain manageable

---

Quantum ML solutions should be used strategically, targeting problems where their inherent advantages—exponential speed-ups, high-dimensional data representation, and optimization efficiency—provide a clear benefit over classical approaches. This decision-making framework offers a structured process for evaluating when to adopt quantum methods based on problem characteristics, resource availability, and long-term scalability. As quantum hardware and algorithms continue to mature, this framework can help guide organizations toward integrating quantum computing into their workflows effectively.

Case Study: Hybrid Classical-Quantum Models – Bridging Two Worlds for Optimized Performance

Hybrid classical-quantum models represent a synergistic approach to solving complex computational problems, leveraging the strengths of both classical and quantum paradigms. By combining the computational efficiency and scalability of classical machine learning (ML) techniques with the unique capabilities of quantum algorithms—such as superposition, entanglement, and quantum parallelism—hybrid models are designed to tackle problems that are either intractable or computationally expensive for purely classical methods. This case study explores the implementation, advantages, and real-world applications of hybrid classical-quantum models, focusing on their ability to optimize performance for high-dimensional, complex tasks.

---

1. Conceptual Overview of Hybrid Classical-Quantum Models

Hybrid models integrate classical and quantum components into a unified computational pipeline:

- **Classical Component:** Handles data preprocessing, feature extraction, and high-level decision-making tasks.
- **Quantum Component:** Addresses computational bottlenecks such as feature mapping, optimization, or solving linear systems of equations.
- **Integration:** The two components interact iteratively, with classical systems feeding data into quantum processors and using quantum outputs to refine models or predictions.

This architecture is particularly advantageous in the era of noisy intermediate-scale quantum (NISQ) devices, where quantum systems are not yet capable of handling end-to-end tasks independently.

---

2. Framework for Developing Hybrid Models

2.1 Problem Decomposition

Hybrid models are most effective when the problem is decomposable into sub-tasks that align with the strengths of classical and quantum systems. For example:

- **Classical Sub-Tasks:** Data cleaning, dimensionality reduction, and initial model training.
- **Quantum Sub-Tasks:** Feature mapping, solving high-dimensional optimization problems, or computing kernel matrices.

2.2 Data Encoding into Quantum States

Data from classical sources must be encoded into quantum states for processing by quantum algorithms. Common encoding methods include:

- **Amplitude Encoding:** Efficiently encodes large datasets by representing data in the amplitudes of quantum states.
- **Basis Encoding:** Maps data into qubits using binary representation.
- **Angle Encoding:** Encodes data features into qubit rotation angles for quantum gates.

2.3 Iterative Feedback Loop

The hybrid model often employs an iterative loop where classical ML algorithms are refined based on outputs from quantum algorithms. For instance:

- A classical model identifies initial clusters in data.
- A quantum algorithm optimizes the cluster centroids or calculates similarity metrics using quantum-enhanced techniques.
- The classical model adjusts its parameters based on quantum outputs and re-evaluates predictions.

---

3. Real-World Applications of Hybrid Classical-Quantum Models

3.1 Application in Portfolio Optimization

- **Problem:** Optimizing a portfolio of assets under multiple constraints (e.g., risk, return, and diversification).
- **Classical Role:** Uses historical data to estimate covariance matrices and calculate initial weights.
- **Quantum Role:** Implements the Quantum Approximate Optimization Algorithm (QAOA) to find optimal asset allocations.
- **Outcome:** The hybrid model balances computational efficiency and accuracy, outperforming purely classical approaches in scenarios with a large number of assets and constraints.

3.2 Application in Image Recognition

- **Problem:** Classifying high-resolution images with millions of features.
- **Classical Role:** Uses convolutional neural networks (CNNs) for initial feature extraction.
- **Quantum Role:** Applies quantum kernel methods to enhance classification accuracy by capturing complex feature interactions.
- **Outcome:** Improved performance, particularly in identifying subtle patterns or anomalies.

3.3 Application in Drug Discovery

- **Problem:** Identifying potential drug candidates by simulating molecular interactions.

- **Classical Role:** Filters large chemical databases to identify promising molecules.
- **Quantum Role:** Uses Variational Quantum Eigensolver (VQE) to simulate molecular interactions with high accuracy.
- **Outcome:** Accelerated drug discovery pipeline with reduced computational overhead.

---

4. Implementation Workflow: A Step-by-Step Guide

1. **Problem Analysis:**
    - Define the computational bottlenecks and decide which tasks can benefit from quantum acceleration.
2. **Data Preparation:**
    - Preprocess the data using classical methods and encode it into quantum-compatible formats.
3. **Quantum Algorithm Design:**
    - Select quantum algorithms suitable for the task (e.g., QAOA for optimization, qPCA for dimensionality reduction).
4. **Hybrid Integration:**
    - Develop interfaces between classical and quantum systems using frameworks like TensorFlow Quantum or Qiskit Aqua.
5. **Model Training and Evaluation:**
    - Train the hybrid model iteratively, using quantum outputs to refine classical predictions.
6. **Performance Benchmarking:**
    - Compare the hybrid model's performance against classical baselines using metrics like accuracy, runtime, and scalability.

---

5. Advantages of Hybrid Classical-Quantum Models

- **Enhanced Efficiency:** Quantum algorithms accelerate computationally intensive tasks like matrix inversion or optimization.
- **Improved Accuracy:** Quantum methods capture complex data relationships that classical algorithms may overlook.

- **Scalability:** Hybrid models leverage classical systems for large-scale tasks, reducing the burden on limited quantum hardware.
- **Robustness:** Iterative feedback between classical and quantum components improves overall model robustness.

---

6. Challenges and Mitigation Strategies

6.1 Quantum Hardware Limitations

- **Challenge:** Limited qubit count and susceptibility to noise in NISQ devices.
- **Solution:** Employ error mitigation techniques and hybrid architectures to offload less critical tasks to classical systems.

6.2 Data Encoding Overheads

- **Challenge:** Encoding large datasets into quantum states can be resource-intensive.
- **Solution:** Use efficient encoding schemes (e.g., amplitude encoding) and dimensionality reduction techniques.

6.3 Algorithm Integration Complexity

- **Challenge:** Designing seamless interactions between classical and quantum algorithms.
- **Solution:** Use hybrid ML frameworks like PennyLane or TensorFlow Quantum for streamlined development.

---

7. Future Potential of Hybrid Models

As quantum hardware evolves, hybrid classical-quantum models will increasingly dominate domains requiring high-dimensional computation and rapid optimization. They are expected to play a transformative role in fields such as:

- **Autonomous Systems:** Enhancing decision-making and navigation in self-driving vehicles.
- **Energy Management:** Optimizing power grids and renewable energy resources.
- **Advanced Cybersecurity:** Strengthening cryptographic methods and intrusion detection systems.

Hybrid classical-quantum models represent a pivotal step in the evolution of machine learning, enabling organizations to harness the strengths of quantum computing without abandoning the reliability and scalability of classical methods. By strategically integrating quantum algorithms into classical ML pipelines, these models unlock unprecedented computational capabilities, making them indispensable for tackling the most complex challenges across industries. As the quantum ecosystem matures, hybrid solutions will continue to define the cutting edge of innovation in machine learning and beyond.

ABOUT THE AUTHOR

Timothy Ugbaja is a seasoned data scientist, quantum computing advocate, and the visionary CEO of Tilaverse Inc., USA. With a distinguished career spanning more than two decades in technology, education, and data science, Timothy brings a unique fusion of academic rigor and practical industry expertise to the frontier of innovation.

He served as a computer science lecturer for over 14 years, shaping future IT professionals while mastering emerging technologies across artificial intelligence, machine learning, and cloud computing. His professional journey extends beyond academia, with more than 20 years of hands-on experience in cutting-edge domains such as Snowflake, Spark, Qubole, R, Python, DevOps, and most recently, quantum machine learning.

A prolific thought leader, Timothy has authored more than 60 industry articles that cover the intersections of Cloud Computing, Data Science, Software Engineering, and Quantum Technologies. His career includes impactful roles such as IT Manager at Scot Longman City of London Ambassadors Ltd. and DevOps Consultant at Odyssey Educational Foundation, where he spearheaded advanced projects in data pipeline architecture, machine learning, and scalable cloud analytics.

Timothy is also the author of ***Cloud Data Science Mastery: Unlocking Snowflake's Power with Spark, R, Qubole, and Python***, a definitive guide for professionals aiming to thrive in the era of cloud-based data science. With ***The Power of Quantum Machine Learning with TensorFlow Quantum, Qiskit, PennyLane, and Amazon Braket: From Algorithms to Applications***, he extends his expertise to the rapidly evolving field of quantum computing, offering a roadmap for researchers, practitioners, and innovators eager to unlock the transformative potential of quantum machine learning.

As both a leader and an educator, Timothy Ugbaja continues to push the boundaries of technology while inspiring the next generation of scientists, engineers, and entrepreneurs to embrace the future of quantum-powered intelligence.

www.ingramcontent.com/pod-product-compliance
Lightning Source LLC
LaVergne TN
LVHW071412210926
848486LV00004B/261